A Wild, Rank Place

A WILD,
RANK PLACE

❧ ❧ ❧ ❧ ❧ ❧ ❧ ❧ ❧ ❧ ❧ ❧ ❧

One Year on Cape Cod

David Gessner

UNIVERSITY PRESS OF NEW ENGLAND Hanover and London

This book was acquired and developed by the Center for American Places, of Harrisonburg, Virginia, and Mesilla, New Mexico, for publication by University Press of New England.

University Press of New England, Hanover, NH 03755
Printed in the United States of America
5 4 3 2 1
CIP data appear at the end of the book

Some of the names of characters have been changed.

"Killing Fathers" originally appeared in *Kinesis*. "June" originally appeared as "A June Journal" in *Creative Nonfiction*.

All drawings are by the author.
The drawing on page 46 of a man clamming
is based on a photograph that appeared in
The Cape Naturalist, vol. 15, no. 1 (Summer 1986): 5.

It is a wild, rank place, and there is no flattery in it.

THOREAU, *Cape Cod*

To my father,

David Marshall Gessner

1937–1994

Contents

Acknowledgments

First and foremost, I would like to thank my wife, the writer Nina de Gramont. Not only did she support, love, and tolerate me during the building of this book, but she played a pivotal role in shaping it, challenging me with her editor's pen to expand by condensing. She has also, I am happy to say, grown to share my passion for Cape Cod.

This book was written and conceived under the difficult circumstances of my father's illness and death. I can't say enough about the strength and support of my entire family, Scott, Jenny, and, in particular, Heidi and my mother, Barbara, who, despite all the evidence to the contrary, has always believed.

On Cape Cod I could always rely on my second family, the Schadts. The Cape also brings to mind two close friends. It was with David Rotman that I first spent an off-season on the Cape, and the memories of that strange, difficult, and wonderful year have been with me ever since. And, of course, I can't think of the Cape without thinking of Hones. Mark Honerkamp, a best friend to so many of us, rivals my father in filling the Cape house with a Rabelaisian love of life. But beneath his beer-swilling, meat-grilling exterior, I know he shares my love and appreciation of this particular wild, rank place.

Back in Colorado, where much of the real work of revising was done, I was fortunate to be part of a writing community that was presided over by Janet Hard and included Karen Auvinen, Heidi Krauth, Burns Ellison, Jim Campbell, and fellow "Mountain Palace" writers Melinda MacInnis and Mark Spitzer. For most of us in this group Reg Saner has been there steadily as guide and occasional father figure, always available, encouraging, and full of grace.

Finally I would like to thank George F. Thompson, president of the Center for American Places, for the original confidence he showed in the book and for the hard work he put in to help me present it in its current form.

August 1996   D.G.

A Wild, Rank Place

PRELUDE
The Return

↓

Fall. The best time on the Cape. Today one of those cool, almost cold, mornings when the wind gets things going. It wakes me by slamming the loosened shutters against the house. Then, while I stretch in bed, it puts on a puppet show, pulsing cornrows of light against the dark oak planks of the bedroom wall.

Here the wind never rests. It blusters about the neck, driving out summer, spreading the stench of the sea. You can watch it churning around the house like paint whorls on a van Gogh. It rises up the hill and buffets the walls, dings halyards on masts, sets the trees shaking.

I pull on a flannel shirt and head out to the back deck. I walk to the edge of the vegetation, unzip, and water the crawlers and bayberry. The wind gusts and eddies, rustles the half-shaded leaves. After two years in the dry interior West, this is what I need. A place that smells of low tide. Of seaweed and skate eggs. Air that is thick with salt.

A bright crimson, half-devoured carcass of a field mouse lies on the front lawn. Young greenflies feast. I hike down the hill for the paper and stare back up at the gray house that sits on top of a small hill, overwhelmed by its surroundings. Some day I expect to return from the beach to find the house swallowed whole by the weeds or sinking deep into the earth. The moat of oak, a single pear tree, cedar, and pitch pine that once protected my family's privacy now closes in with claustrophobic intensity. Ivy crawls up the walls. It has hooked its green fingers over the black tar roof shingles, and threatens to pull the entire frame back down into the ground. On the side of the house, mangy olive-colored shrubs scrape against the windows and scratch at the kitchen door. Weeds break through the patio.

The house is tired. It slumps and looks its age. Its sidewall shingles suit it perfectly, grayed by the weather, expanding and contracting as the walls wheeze and heave. On the roof are mussels and clumps of dung dropped by gulls. On the old bent antenna mockingbirds gather.

The windows rove absentmindedly. Every time I return I find them in different places—they can't keep still. They look as if they had been placed haphazardly, as if the carpenters who had built them had been too tired—or unprofessional—to finish the job. The only part of the house that still shows any fighting spirit is its ridge, the roof beam. This single board runs below the roof like a spine. As with the ridges of many houses on the Cape, it had been steamed and bowed; it arcs like the back of a frightened cat. Alone it strains against the house's collapse, against the downward pull.

As a spectator of this slow-moving battle, my emotions are mixed. I root for the vegetation, but love the house. I grew up under this roof, and for the next year will once again be a squatter, living and writing, on my father's land.

I walk inside. At night I keep the screen door propped open with a rock, and the wind drives out the insects. But the musty smell is strong, a smell from childhood. The smell inside a box of crayons. And the foul, salt smell of a sailbag opened after winter.

Though I live on the tamer side of the Cape, from here I can look out across the bay, past Provincetown's hook, to the Atlantic. In the Rockies I lived in beautiful places—canyons and parks—but without the ocean. There is a religion, a music, to the waves and water, and today I'm back where I belong. After breakfast, I walk to the beach, my feet speeding straight for the sea.

I walk deliberately into the chilly water, never flinching like a tourist. I dive in and out, pushing up, going under, pushing up again, not really swimming so much as plunging with porpoise dives. Keeping my eyes open, I dive right down to the bottom, where it is coldest. I skim along, my stomach scraping the sea floor, watching a chain link of sunlight range over the green ridges of bottom sand. Suddenly, the greenness, the shoots of gold and sparks of silver, catch me by surprise. I laugh out loud. Bubbles explode through my nose.

I like the fact that farther down the beach a woman wearing a sweater watches me. "Is he crazy?" I imagine her thinking. "It's too cold to swim." There is an element of self-conscious theater in my Cape rituals. I like putting on a show, a show mostly, but not only, for myself.

To live near the ocean again.

The West is beautiful, but my time there was neatly framed by cancer. My own sickness at the beginning of the stay, my father's at the other end, the time in between spent writing about disease. Two weeks ago my last tests, my lipoproteins and final CAT scan, told me I was clean. At that point I knew I had to come here. The Cape for me means health, and today I feel strong, sprung from a cage, ready to conquer the world on my own terms.

"First be a good animal," wrote Emerson. That dictate will guide me through the year. Of course, if the doctors had told me I was going to die, I would have come here anyway. I'd sleep and write and eat. I'd work out fanatically: swimming, walking, running, riding. I'd die in the best shape possible.

This year will be a celebration of health, of recovery, but I'm here also to think about sickness. My father and I are linked by our cancers. We are both aggressive and blunt men. Cancer is the right disease for us. It has an American way of growing. Relentless, rapacious. Cancer attacks; it is ambitious. Cancer believes in manifest destiny. It thinks it deserves everything.

I have heard all the new theories about ways to stop and prevent cancer. Broccoli and phytochemicals, vitamins, avoiding power lines, the need for less aggressive behavior, and on and on and on. I'll take salt water. My cure and prevention. I will swim in it at least one day every month I'm here. Against cancer's frantic behavior, I put the natural progression of the ocean. I'm here to live more like the sea.

My desk sits at the center of the northwest wall, facing out the porthole that overlooks the beach, and, farther east, the harbor. Within reach is a smaller table, a German sidecar of a table piled high with coffee cups, files, folders, and a blue Maxwell House can filled with pens and pencils.

I sip coffee. A fine day. Birds pick the seeds I've spread on the

slope below my window. Two purple finches and a fat baby spar-
row eat nervously. (They start if I so much as reach for my eraser.)
Another finch arrives but keeps its distance from the others, settling in right next to the windowpane. I watch it jabber straight
up at the sky. It's so close I can see its tiny throat vibrate.

Below my desk is a sea-captain's chest filled with old journals,
letters, photos, and high-school yearbooks. I'm tired of fiction, of
wrestling with novels. I have come here to take stock. I will sift
through this chest absentmindedly, trying to define where I've
been, sorting through and collecting past moments. It seems an
orderly task. Controllable. Safe.

But late in the day I am reminded that this year is about more
than collecting old moments. Or, if I am here to collect, it's to
collect new moments as well.

I take an evening walk on the beach. I love the end of day,
when the light fades and dies. The rocks of the bluff change into
hairy, warted gorgons, covered with kelp, periwinkles, and barnacles. I stare as the outgoing tide stains the rocks purple, the color
of horse chestnuts, and the small pools of water in the dents of
their skulls shimmer dark blue and silver.

I smell the dead kelp stink and listen to the barnacles hiss and
breathe. For a few seconds all I hear is this breathing and, just for
those seconds, my brain quiets. A strange tingle of pleasure.

Clean from cancer, it's these moments I crave. These moments
I'm here for. They root time for me. They spill over like a water-
color wash into the rest of existence. They last a second and a
lifetime.

THE THING ITSELF

✛

I come to the Cape to live deliberately. I steal this line from Thoreau just as I've stolen my adventure. For the next months my father's summer home will serve as my cabin. Cape Cod Bay will be my pond.

Thoreau's Cape was wild, but today much of that wildness is covered with video stores and malls. In Colorado the Cape existed only in my mind, romanticized. It was easy to forget the crowded roads and beaches, the polluted aquifer, the Jetskis retching into the water, the high cancer rates on the Upper Cape, the coming outfall pipe promising feces on the beach, the Outermost Condos.

How am I justified in still thinking of this place as wild? *Why do I feel healthy and strong here?* Certainly it's easy enough to get depressed. Just picture the cars, more and more each summer, crawling across the bridge from Boston, New York City, and points beyond. Or the mobs of children who grew up spending summers here, and will soon build houses of their own. On the Cape there isn't the luxury of wide open space (or frequent house-clearing fires), and the houses, once built, mark this narrow land forever. We're a little like the rabbits I see on the lawn, their land crisscrossed by roads, forcing them into smaller and smaller patches of wildness.

Walking the beach this morning I'm reminded again that things have changed. Just ahead, up to my left, looming above the sand, is a fortress of a house. Built since I was last here, the house towers above the older homes that sit more modestly on the land. Of course, it isn't only modest for these homes to lie low, but also smart, since water and wind constantly assault. The pitch pine and scrub oak know it's wise to stay small, as did the old builders. The new house suffers from hubris. It has been painted, though the paint will wear off soon, and it rises up arrogantly, making only a token gesture to Cape architecture with the shingles on its east wall.

If the older homes are organic, low and stout, growing out of the essential necessities of place, this growth is inorganic. The house is a herald, signifying the encroachment of suburbia and its aesthetics. It stands three stories high with an attic, boasting a two-car garage, a pink door, and plate-glass windows everywhere. Twin Jetskis rest on the beach below.

Despite this sight, I feel strong today. I have friends, piously thumping their copies of Edward Abbey's books and spouting eco-sabotage, who would laugh at the notion that this little stretch of beach is "wild." But as I walk this walk I've walked a thousand times before I feel a secret thrill.

Perhaps this points to a tameness in me. On the Cape, unlike in the West, I recognize all the birds—the cardinals and catbirds, plovers and terns, doves and mockingbirds. Back in Colorado, deer are common to the point of nuisance, but here you're blessed if you spy one on the bluff. We Americans romanticize wildness as never before, as anyone romanticizes what is being lost, but it could be that I'm personally better suited to a more domestic wildness. Maybe I should be grateful that the Cape, with its new homes and developments, still feels wild to me. Realistically, we'll soon have to content ourselves with smaller, more European, patches of wildness, as unpleasant as that prospect may sound.

Most of the empty, boarded-up homes are abandoned for the off-season, literally left for the birds. A line of starlings, fat and speckled, roost along the ridge of Bagley's house, the last house on the beach. On this overcrowded planet it's amazing how often I can have this walk to myself. Even during the height of summer few stray beyond the artificial boundaries of the beach. Night or bad weather guarantee solitude. I head toward the spit of rocks below Stone's mansion and break into a wide stupid smile as the bluff comes into view.

Where do I feel more at home than on this beach? Here thoughts are swamped by the smells, sounds, and sights of place. The gentle hypnotic lapping of waves. A prehistoric cormorant on a slick black rock. The delicate lacework of sea-grass roots breaking down through a ledge of sand, the roots light brown, beaded with last night's rainwater. The humanmade and the natural

intertwined. Green gun shells entangled in seaweed, and a Honey Dew Donuts cup ("Always good, Always fresh") housing three snail-like insects. The white chest of a seagull carcass heaving up from the sand, its beak bright red like lipstick. An old lobster trap washed ashore.

Climbing up the side of the bluff, I come upon more abandoned homes. I peer into the dirt tunnels built by swallows. The holes are burrowed into rich orange-brown chunks of rock-sand. A thin line runs down the center of one tunnel, as if a miniature boat had dragged its keel into the lair.

Considering the bluff's erosion, I should turn around and not add to its decay, but on impulse I climb to the top, up over a small ledge of sand between rash-red poison ivy and thorn bushes. I sit on the ledge and face the sea; a gull rises in front of me, wheeling, beating into the wind but getting nowhere, treading air. From this height I can see the entire neck.

There I had got the Cape under me, as much as if I were riding it bare-backed. It was not as on a map, or seen from the stagecoach; but there I found it all out of doors, huge and real, Cape Cod! as it cannot be represented on a map, color it as you will; the thing itself.

I appreciate Thoreau's words, but what I see from this angle is just the opposite. Not the thing itself. From the bluff I look down at the beach, the jetties, the harbor. All of Sesuit looking like a map spread out on my desk.

The thing itself. The phrase has a modern ring, reminiscent of William Carlos Williams and the Imagists, but Thoreau was no stranger to the idea. "Reality is fabulous," he said, "we crave nothing but reality." Emerson was more consistently representative of his time when he wrote: "Every natural fact is emblematic . . . a symbol of some spiritual fact."

Of course, today we are scolded if we make symbols of the landscape. Anthropocentrism is a dirty word. Though more than a closet romantic himself, Edward Abbey sums up the modern naturalist's attitude in the first chapter of *Desert Solitaire*:

> The personification of the natural is exactly the tendency I wish to suppress in myself, to eliminate for good. . . . I want to be able to look at and into a juniper tree, a piece of quartz, a vulture, a spider, and see it as it is in itself, devoid of all humanly ascribed qualities, anti-Kantian, even the categories of scientific description.

Abbey's idea is powerful—the gulls, the bluff, the salt, the bay, all on their own terms—but at the same time I have my reservations. Theoretically, it's hard to fault seeing things "as they are," but how often do we really approach the important landscapes in our lives this way? It can be argued that this idealization of a non-romantic view is a modern romanticism in its own right. How can humans approach a thing without their minds constantly coloring and distorting? And do we really desire "the thing itself"? I delight in the fact that I can look down at the neck and see it as a map. I'm reminded of the map at the beginning of the Winnie the Pooh books—drawings of Piglet's house, Rabbit's hole, the honey tree. It's the same for me. Each spot I see has a story connected with it. Often several stories.

The modern prejudice against the romantic isn't entirely honest. When I look at the neck it seems at once smaller and larger than it actually is. Romanticizing is as natural as breathing, and, at times, as healthy. Our minds have minds of their own. Reality is fabulous, yes, but we also crave something more. Symbol, perhaps. Meaning.

~

I push up from my seat on the bluff's edge. Rather than an erosion-aiding slide down the cliff front, I decide to exit inland, picking my way through the poison ivy and briars of Stone's backyard. Once I've escaped private property, I hike over to Old Town Lane. Recently, a wealthy widow died and her children sold the land along the street as subdivided lots. When I was growing up the road was a tunnel of honey locusts, the most interesting of the Cape's winter trees. They looked like giant mushroom stems, dry and brittle and twisted, woven with greens and blues. Now many of the locusts have been cut down for the new lots. According to recent Cape logic the next step will be to rename the street Locust Lane. Lately those who destroy Cape Cod like to sound quaint and old-fashioned. They rip out a pine grove with bulldozers, then call the street Old Pine Grove. They do the same with Fox's Den, Cranberry Way, and Oak Bluff. All once were what they now are called.

I return home. The house looks like a living thing, growing out of the ground. For the rest of my family, it is a summer playhouse, but this isn't the first time I'll fortify it for winter, dragging a woodstove into the living room and tacking galleon sails of plastic insulation to the windows. Then, when the cold winds come and the plastic thwucks in and out, filling and falling, the house becomes a ship.

It's true I romanticize the house. And why not? Here I first read *Moby Dick* as the flagpole's shackles dinged in the background and wind battered the walls. Here I hunched over my drawings and battled mano a mano with Ronald Reagan, swearing that I'd become a great political cartoonist. Here I had my only fling and dated my first love. Here I became a carpenter. Here I ate mushrooms and stared madly into the fire. Here I clutched my copy of *Walden* as if it were the Bible, turning to it for guidance as I lived my own year in the woods.

These were my adventures—admittedly adolescent, internal, and lacking originality—but for me adventures nonetheless. How can I ever hope to see this house objectively? Like all the best places, it is layered with memory. The layers help deepen the love, as in human relationships. I might say I love the canyon in New Mexico where I backpacked for a day or two, but that emotion is different from what I feel for this house, this beach and bluff. The former is more a fling, a one-night stand. It's important that I can close my eyes and see the brown-purple bluff from earlier today, but more important that I can also summon pictures of the bluff in other seasons: lit up by goldenrod, the deep maroon of later fall, the full island bloom of spring. Once I even dreamed of the bluff, saw it there in my sleep, huge and dark and vivid.

We are constant mythmakers, like squirrels building nests. Isn't falling in love making the object of love larger than it is? Or is it just the opposite—seeing a thing *as* it is? To me, the latter seems a more romantic idea. How much of love and friendship is conscious illusion, a going outward, a marriage of imagination and fact? We reach out with what we have, with our knowledge, imagination, affection, memories. How much of Emerson's discovery of his symbols was a result of the ardor of his search, what Keats called "the greeting of the spirit"?

And so now I return to add new layers, new myths. Perhaps I will see the Cape more maturely, with clearer eyes, but I know that this adventure, like my past adventures, is a self-conscious one. I've come here not only to live and walk the beach, but to write about living and walking. Further complicating things, Thoreau's footsteps have not yet washed away from the sand where I walk. He spent three short weeks on the Cape but has claimed it forever. "Suet" he called this neck. Sesuit is its proper name, but Thoreau's mistake may linger longer.

Writing about this land intimidates me. Cape Cod is overdeveloped in more than one sense. It's among the most populated areas on the literary map. In his introduction to Henry Beston's *The Outermost House*, Robert Finch writes:

> Over the centuries an extraordinary number of essayists, poets, and novelists have written about this suggestive landscape. Few, if any, natural areas of comparable size on the continent have been written about as extensively or well.

The fact is Thoreau and others have permanently altered what I see. Their quotes are as much a part of the landscape as the bayberry bushes, and I can't consciously uneducate myself. My adventure is imaginatively filled out by adventures past, my life here partly plagiarism. How much does my knowledge of Thoreau alone in his cabin inform my time in my own? How much of my love of this place was born of books?

I'm left with a small and silly self-portrait. Here I sit in my tamed, wild place. I live alone in a book-filled cabin, talking to ghosts, trying to live a year in the woods at this late date, on this overwritten and contaminated ground.

But it's simpler than that. This is my land, too. I love Cape Cod. There, I've said it. Plainly and clearly and truly. I shake my head and walk outside the house. A moat of vegetation surrounds me. The leaves dance, agitated: bayberry, the oily leaves of the post oak, the honeysuckle, the goldenrod, the poison ivy with its angry red. Silver and shade flicker. Silver on the unkempt grass, silver beyond in the choppy surf. From the deck the eelgrass looks like Christmas tinsel—pure silver strands. Terns fly over the deck, their shadows cross before my feet. The outlines of scrub oak dance on the lawn.

For a moment my mind empties. Perhaps my situation is not so hopelessly confusing. I come to this place with my cluttered head, my past, my ghosts, my books, my delusions, and I reach out with what I have. Like other relationships, my relationship with this place is imperfect, complex. But that doesn't mean it can't provide joy. I remember a line from a book of Cape folklore called *The Narrow Land*. I read it on the plane coming back here, read about the Nauset Indians, how they lived before the white man came:

> They beat their drums in the night on the highlands of Nauset. They lifted their arms to the yellow dawn, and prayed for corn and strong sons. . . . They were the first lords of the Narrow Land, and no other owners of the seaward peninsula have experienced their intimacy of possession.

That is my unreal dream for the year ahead. To reach out with my imagination, to greet the landscape, and—yes—to love it, whatever that means. I know I come late and self-consciously. But secretly, vainly perhaps, I hope to become a lord of the narrow land. To experience intimacy.

THE STINKHORN

✦

This is the right time of year for walking through the marsh. But this morning it came to me. I was expecting company, though not this gamy sort. The wind blew from the north, bringing the briny odor of Spartina grass into my bedroom. The marsh begins less than seventy yards from my house. Beach heather grows on the hill to the east of the harbor where a hundred years before they launched clipper ships. If I lie still in bed and listen hard enough I can hear the sibilant hissing of reeds and saltwater cord grass. It's somehow reassuring having the marsh as a next-door neighbor. People talk about our need for nature; needing a place that is *other* than human. The marsh is more other than most. More primitive and wild.

How do real-estate developers perceive these bits of low-lying wetlands with their vague borders? Their first impulse is to fill them in. Land must be divided, cut into sections with clear boundaries, used. But here is the most primal of landscapes, plagued by greenflies and ticks, protected by smells and strangeness. Developers react as a landlord would finding a caveman in his condo. The marsh is the antirational. Not hell, really. More a place that doesn't fit into our cosmologies at all.

Adults rarely visit the marsh. I remember walking through it as a child with my friend Henry Kirkendall. We spent hours bouncing over the spongy mattress of roots, hiding in the grasses that grew far above our heads. On the way back to the house, I ran through some reeds and—*thwuck*—was sucked in. I sank into the black, rootless muck, down to my ankles, to my knees. I called for Kirk. Scenes from Tarzan movies flashed through my mind, and I knew I'd be sucked all the way down, over my head. I yelled in panic, but this wasn't quicksand. I stopped sinking at my hips, and wrestled my way out, my shoes sucked off and lost in the process. Then I returned home barefoot, black, and reeking, and hosed myself down behind the house. My mother looked at my clothes and slowly shook her head.

~

The marsh takes up a good portion of Sesuit neck. I like the rising and dipping of the word "Sesuit," but prefer Thoreau's misnomer—Suet, the hard fatty tissues around the kidneys of cattle and sheep, used in cooking and making tallow. A good, pungent name.

This morning I search Thoreau's journals to see what he wrote about marshes. I don't find what I'd hoped for, but a little glimpse of graffiti catches my eye:

I read the entry accompanying the drawing. On October 16, 1856, Thoreau wrote of this "rare and remarkable fungus":

> The whole height six and three quarters inches, two thirds of it being buried in the sphagnum. One of the fungus named *impudicus*, I think. In all respects a most disgusting object, yet very suggestive.

As he guessed, the mushroom was the *Phallus impudicus*, the common stinkhorn. He goes on to describe it in great tactile detail—"the whole plant frail and trembling"—and gives extensive measurements, obviously after handling the fungus a good deal.

Continuing his description, Thoreau betrays two sides of his personality. First, a sentence of raw physical detail: "It smelled like a dead rat in the ceiling, in all the ceilings of the house." Spoken like a man who wasn't afraid of getting his hands dirty, who once said he'd eaten a fried rat with good relish. But in the next sentence Henry the Sunday-school teacher takes over. "Pray what was nature thinking of when she made this?" he asks. "She almost puts herself on a level with those who draw in privies."

Thoreau the crude versus Thoreau the prude. It's an interesting fight. For a ringside seat, just open to *Walden*'s "Higher Laws" chapter. Henry's dainty shudders rise off the page as he bemoans our "reptile and sensual life." But if we tire of this schoolmarm railing against the sins of the flesh, we can flip back to the chapter's opening paragraph. Here we find Thoreau the eater of fried rats and the mucker in muck. Here is the famous woodchuck mugger, so aroused by a furry rodent that he feels "a strange thrill of savage delight," and is "strongly tempted to devour him raw; not that I was hungry then, except for the wildness he represented."

Savage delight.

~

Though I'd planned on spending the day exploring the marsh, Thoreau distracts me. This contradiction in Henry David interests me for a personal reason. It reminds me of my father, and of this house.

My father is a crude man fighting it out with his own inner puritan. Bald, with a proud chest and large stomach, his rumbling voice and strong simian features dominated my childhood. And it was here, in this house during summers on the Cape, that the contradictions in his personality revealed themselves.

By day he was a workaholic. Vacation meant toil. He was the first one awake. Cleaning. Loudly doing the dishes, emptying and reemptying the same empty trash can. As he worked he bit the corners of his lips, his brow furrowed, as if some interior screws had been tightened and tightened beyond the point of stripping. "Life is maintenance," he told me. He believed it. Driven, he said little during the day, but worked and worked, looking on the rest of us with judging eyes.

But the nights were different: he drank bottles of red wine and changed. My mother tried to shepherd him in with cries of "*Dave*-id," but he grew blunt and wild. Vulgar, too. Among friends he spoke his mind, offending some, delighting others.

Why did he drink? In these times of rehab clinics and Alcoholics Anonymous, the only proper answer is physical addiction. But I'm convinced there was something more—in part, the simple release of inhibitions. A man who thought all day, who burdened himself with his concerns and the concerns of others could be forgiven if he wanted a time of thoughtlessness and irresponsibility. And he found something else in drink: exhilaration. A chance, in a compromised world, of letting out an uncompromised hoot of joy, of certainty. A chance to cut through the day to day nonsense, to cut through—to use one of his favorite words—the bullshit.

During my late adolescence my father and I had an unusual way of being close. The first time it happened was after a night of drinking, but soon it became a simple ritual. We would leave the house together, walk outside, and piss off the back deck.

It was usually late in the evening when we strolled into the darkness. The deck was a raft floating out on the brambles and bayberry, and we described our arcs into nature while he described the world for me.

I would stand there staring at his bulging bullfrog eyes and the shine of moonlight like oil on his bald head.

"She's a beauty," he said to me one night, pointing up to the yellow "Don't Tread on Me" flag that snapped in the wind above our heads.

"She sure is," I said.

"That my friend," he declared, "is a varsity flag."

My father ranked everything. Our cat was a varsity cat. Our dog decidedly j.v.

We finished our business and zipped up, walked back to the deck. He was silent for a while; then he pointed up at the sky.

"Do you know what's up there?" he asked. His voice boomed.

"The flag?" I guessed.

"No, my friend," he said. "That's the sky . . . the universe."

He made a broad sweeping gesture with his arms that encompassed both the universe and our yard. He smiled. A king surveying his realm. He pounded his chest and snorted in the salt air.

"This is it, my friend," he said. "This is something."

He walked over to where I stood, wrapped an arm around me, and pulled me into his chest. His odor was rank, familiar. Red wine stained his mouth like ghastly lipstick.

"I love you, David," he said. "You know I love you."

Only after drinking could he say those words. Even then they came out thick, as if his tongue were coated with glue. I nodded.

"I love you," he said, "but you're crazy."

"What do you mean?" I asked, more curious than insulted.

"Not in a bad way. No, no, good crazy. You're *good crazy*."

I waited for more. He made a smacking noise and puckered his mouth. Then he lumbered across the deck and into the house, letting the screen door thwack shut behind him.

I laugh at the men's movement, at sweat lodges and drumming, but that was the closest I've ever felt to my father. His strange pagan appreciation of the world and nature forged a bond between us. Later, at college, when walking home drunk late at night, I would stop at a particular oak and mark my territory. "I have watered the red huckleberry, the sand cherry and the nettle tree," wrote Thoreau. Me too. To this day I insist there was something religious about the experience.

Pulling my head out of Thoreau's journals, I walk outside. I stand on the back deck and breathe in the low-tide smells of the marsh. The whispering of the reeds and grasses grows louder. I have been alone here for a month now and am going slightly crazy. Megalomania muscles out other parts of my psyche. I'm convinced the things I'm working on are tremendously important.

> Once or twice, however, while I lived at the pond, I found myself ranging the woods, like a half-starved hound, with a strange abandonment, seeking some kind of venison which I might devour, and no morsel could have been too savage for me.

I pull a small plastic bag from my pocket, open it, and stare at the contents. The stalks and the stems of the mushrooms are dry and brittle, gnarled and twisted like miniature locust trees. I have no right eating these. It makes no sense. I'm thirty-two years old, long past seeking revelations in drugs, and have had my share of health problems. But I know I'll eat them anyway. I make several promises to myself: I will do these drugs as an adult, will take notes and avoid the self-obsession of adolescence, will try to be objective about this most subjective of experiences.

That resolved, I gobble a stem. Immediately, my stomach rebels. I grind up the rest using a spoon and a clean ashtray as mortar and pestle. Then I mix it with peanut butter and eat it in a sandwich.

Twenty minutes later my thoughts are skittering. Everything—particularly my clock radio—seems ridiculously funny. I root through my clothes, searching for a notebook. Finally, I find it and clutch it to my chest. I run out the front door. I listen as my work boots clomp up the hill, a reverberating sound on the pavement, like horseshoes, echoing off the house.

I stop at the top of the hill and try to speak but sputter meaninglessly. This strikes me as absurd and I laugh out loud. Then a whooshing noise, a sound like the soughing of wind through the tops of trees—only louder, somehow different. Recognition: the sound is a car turning the corner. I panic . . . I can't seem to move. I stand there frozen with fear, unable to speak, blubbering like a village idiot, terrified that one of my neighbors might find me and want to stop and talk.

Before the car turns the corner I run off the side of the road through a small opening in the briars, down a path the dogs use. I run, hunched over, along the path, then stop and stare ahead, my mouth hung open like a big dumb bass. A beautiful brown and gold world surrounds me. Twigs and brush crunch underfoot. I destroy entire miniature communities with each giant footstep. A thorn cuts my cheek. I taste my own blood, smear it on my face. I'm still laughing, staring down into my hand at the unreal and pasty blood, when I reach the clearing. I forget my cut and try to take everything in . . . brown and gray . . . a comfortable floor of twigs and dead leaves . . . wet mulch . . . a rotting scrub oak crawling with ants . . . an ancient Schlitz can turned green by the weather . . . a furless tennis ball . . . a faded blue Filet-O-Fish container, gaping upward, as if hungry. . . .

I pull myself away. The path cuts down a hill and I follow. Now I'm oriented and know where to go. The smell pulsing up the path is briny, almost sexual. I head toward the marsh.

"If you can't screw, you can't write," said a colleague of Mircea Eliade. Fearing impotence, he was sure his pen would dry up, too.

Thoreau wrote quite well without screwing. By the end of his career he put stock in something like the old theory once propagated by boxing trainers. For years women were kept away from training camps because it was supposed that if a boxer had sex he would "lose his legs." Thoreau held a similar belief: chastity aids creativity. He wrote that "the generative energy, which, when we are loose, dissipates and makes us unclean, when we are continent, invigorates and inspires us." And: "There is a copulative and generative force of love behind every effort destined to be successful."

With no human outlet, it was into his journal that Thoreau poured his seed. And into nature. "I confess that it excites me," he said of a cranberry bog. "I love it as a maiden." He admitted the fullness of pokeweed aroused him. And professed love for a shrub oak.

Of course, the Freudians have a field day with this. They replace the picture of the earthy Thoreau—the wheelbarrow trundler and rat eater—with a new prim and sexless model, frightened of flesh. This is the Thoreau who cringes at the "slimy bestial life." This Thoreau isn't comfortable with the messy, the sticky, and why should he be? Why be comfortable with something he never experienced, or experienced in only a limited or guilty way?

For my part, I believe strongly in the transmutation of sex into creativity. In 1991, a tumor was found in my right testicle. An orchiectomy was performed, the testicle removed. I was assured that mine was the best type of cancer possible, and underwent radiation treatment for a month. The cancer hasn't returned, and I'm told it's unlikely it will. But there have been other complications. My remaining testicle is wrapped round by a substantial varicocele—veins that fill my scrotum, in the words of my doctor, like "a bag of worms." These veins are tiny tree roots circling my spermatic cord, and the heat they create diminishes the motility of my sperm. In other words, I can't reproduce.

Two months after I learned this news, I broke up with my girlfriend of eight years and moved to Colorado. The first week in Colorado was spent unpacking my things, moving into a small cottage beneath spectacular walls of red sandstone. Then I began to write. And write. A novel about cancer poured out of me. At the same time I took notes on my new home and began to sketch out a draft of another book.

Even that wasn't enough. My head overheated. What I really wanted was to write five or six books at the same time, like Dostoyevsky with a hundred plots in his brain, working on one novel in the morning, another at night. I'd never felt so creative, so, pardon the pun, potent. It was as if my body were talking to me: saying, one way or another, I *will* procreate.

In the late eighties my father's drinking began to be considered a problem. There was talk of an "intervention." My sister convinced me to help her confront him. Since I was older, she elected me to do the talking. After cramming for three days with literature Heidi supplied (*Bradshaw on Family*, AA brochures, *Codependent No More!*), I felt ready.

My father sat at his desk in front of us while I preached to him.

He listened quietly to my words. He didn't even nod in reply, and my confidence slipped. I sounded to my own ears like the most self-righteous of teetotalers.

"I just feel that it hurts you so much," I said. "It seems as if you'd be much happier if you cut out the drinking. You could get into a support group. Your friends would respect you for it and Heidi and I would be so proud. . . ."

I rambled on for ten minutes, by far the longest speech I'd ever addressed to my father. He kept his eyes on me the whole time, barely blinking, and when I finally finished talking I felt foolish. He paused for a long dramatic minute before replying. Then he looked me squarely in the eyes.

"That's all fine and well, David," he said. "But I'd rather die than stop drinking."

I nodded.

I knew exactly what he meant.

I've read that when salt marshes are polluted to the point where the water becomes anaerobic, the marsh starts to smell of hydrogen sulfide, a smell like rotting eggs. But even healthy marshes reek. It's a scent that my Colorado friends wouldn't like much. Offensive, almost lewd. You have to get used to it. The smell of the ocean is strong, but this is ocean smell squared. An appalling but pleasing perfume like the odor of toe jam.

Now, entering the marsh, I crash down through the tick-infested grass into another world. The water is a vivid blue—an indescribable blue—against the dead brown and drab green. Chocolate heads of sedge grass rustle like crumpling paper, and the marshland is spongy beneath my feet. I'm walking on a trampoline, walking on the moon. I bounce along sucking in the rank, peat smell.

Down closer to the water, the marsh floor is less matted; the roots weaving below loosen their grip. This is the mud that pulls you down like quicksand, but I challenge the marsh. I crash recklessly through the Spartina grass until my pants and sneakers soak through. I love the mud's cold squish and ooze. How appropriate that this primitive muck was born of a glacier. Sloshing along, I feel like I'm moving back through time. I hear a noise. A raccoon? A deer? A cormorant? I stand still, knee-deep in the mud, waiting for something to move. Truthfully, I wouldn't be surprised by anything . . . Perhaps a pterodactyl flying up over the sedge.

The marsh is not linear. It fights progress. It has no boundaries.

These days it's easy to decry the effects of progress. But think of the prescience of Thoreau. With America charging west, building, bustling, barely able to contain itself, and with the country's natural resources seemingly inexhaustible, he warned that there was not enough wildness left. To most people, this must have sounded like the ranting of a lunatic.

In 1849—the same year that Thoreau made his first trip to Cape Cod—Asa, Paul, and David Shiverick got together with Christopher Hall, a retired shipmaster and owner, and created the Shiverick Shipyard. For the next fourteen years clipper ships were built in East Dennis, less than a hundred feet from my house. They were built with reckless energy: eight ships over fourteen years, all launched from the small hill above the marsh.

I learned about the shipyard from a pamphlet written by Nancy Devita, a painter and co-owner of a local art gallery who died of cancer in 1986. My mother tells me she was a beautiful woman; I know she wrote beautifully about the ships. They were three-masters, square-rigged, one thousand to fifteen hundred tons. It's hard to picture clipper ships almost two hundred feet long sliding down my neighbor's backyards. The shipbuilders, most from East Dennis, experienced a burst of productivity rivaling any builders in the world. The boats were among the finest that sailed: *The Hippogriffe, Kit Carson, Webfoot, Ellen Sears, Christopher Hall,* and, finally, *The Belle of the West.* Nancy Devita's pamphlet tells me that the last is "still considered one of the most beautiful ships ever built." From East Dennis, these ships left for San Francisco, Calcutta, Samoa.

Think of the noise, the clutter, the frenzied activity during those fourteen years. I can see the docks, the caulking area, the saw pit, the blacksmith shop. Using a mallet and gouge, carpenters built the half model for the ship before building the ship itself. They made the chalk lines on the floor, fitting the wooden templates that served as models for the ship's ribs. The workers lived in shacks on Quivet neck and crossed the harbor on a now long-forgotten wooden walkway across the marsh, crossing over every morning, hammers in hand.

I spent my first winter after college on the Cape, and it amazed me that all this had happened so close to my home. It isn't overstatement to say the idea set my imagination aflame. Working on a novel, I looked to the production of clipper ships for inspiration. The window next to where I wrote pointed toward the old shipyard site. "Produce books as they did ships," said the note card tacked over my desk.

Which leads to another conflict. The romance of productivity versus the romance of wildness. To think like Thoreau, that material progress is bad, is a hard thing for an American. We're an ant colony. We love to produce! To build! I spent the winters while I tried to write my novel working as a carpenter. I hated the fact that more and more houses were being built on the land I loved, but there were times I loved the actual building. Cape Cod in winter reminds me of earlier times, and the men I worked with were descendants of shipbuilders. The same frenzied energy that went into the building of clipper ships was apparent during the eighties' building boom on the Cape. But now the energy was turned inward. And as we built we were killing the spirit we built with, and changing forever the wildness of the land.

The noise isn't a pterodactyl, but close. On the other side of the cord grass a great blue heron patiently sits. I stand still and study it. Mussed hair, pale face, gray with black streaks, black shoulder patch. It keeps still, down periscope, a bulky gray torpid heap, hardly moving for ten minutes. It finally unfolds its neck into a muscular question mark and slowly looks about, turning like a weather vane in a light breeze. Then a startling moment. All of the sudden it stretches its neck up to its full height, up and up to the sky like a sun worshiper. Its bulk was an illusion. Stretched out, the bird is razor thin, its neck long and breakable, its legs twiglike and knobby-kneed.

It stays stretched out for a few minutes and then gradually—

very gradually—lets its neck fold down onto itself, accordioning into its chest, returning to the illusion of bulk. So patient, but at the same time so many changes of posture. It opens its mouth wide and shakes its head. I want to reach out and stroke the gray felt of its neck, the gray sheen of its back.

As if my mind and feet are one, I step forward clumsily and crunch down on grassy stalks. The heron lifts and flies off with two powerful flaps.

Exhilarated, I follow a canal deeper into the marsh. Crabs scuttle underfoot. Red-winged blackbirds land on reeds. The reeds brush up against each other like the wool suits of Sunday school children. Sibilant. I discover a marsh wren's nest near a pile of garbage. Sunlight in the woven grasses, long reeds, and silver trash.

Words come back to me. The rediscovery of language. In the middle of the marsh, I mumble to myself like a lunatic. At first my words are clumsy, but gradually I remember how much I like to talk. My tongue loosens. Soon it flaps about wildly, a small fish landed in a rowboat. I talk faster; my words get louder and louder, my mouth never breaks stride. It issues forth a river of words, words running over the beach in streams and freshets.

I barely know what I'm saying, something about how crude the marsh is.

"Not for polite society," I yell to no one. "The marsh is vulgar. Like my father!"

I make connections where none exist. I take mock offense at the marsh and yell out synonyms. A human thesaurus.

"Acrid," I yell. "Gamy, reeking, putrescent, salacious, vulgar."

I might as well be speaking another language. All I can hear is the pure noise of my words, all I can feel is the physical pleasure of moving my tongue.

My clothing is black and foul, but I don't care. I like the muck. I'm sure the fecal Freudians would have a good laugh. And they'd have a point. I am a mud-covered, drugged-up writer wandering the marsh, talking to myself.

But now I remember what I like about mushrooms. They reconnect me to the animal in myself. I take off my shoes and feel the cold squish up between my toes. I spit into a tidal canal.

"Bodily fluids are crucial," I yell out loud. I am loose in the marsh. Sweating, breathing, pissing, running, jumping.

Then there was Thoreau's one meeting with Whitman. Bronson Alcott observed that they were like "two wild beasts, each wondering what the other would do, whether to snap or run." Wild or not, Thoreau recoiled at the sight of Whitman's bedpan, which Walt left out in plain view as they talked.

Perhaps Whitman was better suited to the stinkhorn than Thoreau. He, after all, was more aware of the connection between the sexual and the creative, and between the sexual and the religious. It was Whitman who wrote of the "poem drooping shy and unseen that I always carry." Maybe he'd be a better companion for walking the marsh.

Twelve years old: I build dams in my cereal bowl with soggy clumps of raisin bran. I watch through the plate-glass dining-room window as he does battle with the vegetation surrounding the house. Here on the Cape, in this unruly house with its unruly weather, my father feels determined to fight for order. I watch as he attacks the lawn, thrusting the mower out into the wilds, fighting an all-out war. Clipping the hedges, he is possessed. He puts the clippers down and begins to tear bare fisted at the weeds that grow through cracks in the patio.

It's a personal fight. He hates the way the weeds break up through the gray, ordered blocks of concrete. Down on his knees, his belly scrapes the cement, the crack of his ass staring back at me. He digs like a madman with his little trowel. He'll rip and pull until he tears out every last grub and root. He smiles in diabolical triumph after yanking out a particularly stubborn one, and stands up and walks toward me.

I quickly look down at my prop, my compost heap of raisin bran, but there is no hiding from my father. He bangs on the window. He stands huge and Buddha-like in his Bermuda shorts, proudly displaying the offending clump of herbage, holding it up like a savage showing off a scalp. I have no idea how to react, while realizing my reaction probably won't matter much. Before I can respond he is scrambling back to his work. The fact is I could probably dance naked across the lawn without him noticing. He is absorbed in his private war. Back on the front where the battle rages.

Sometimes I remember what it was like urinating when I was sick. At the time I was convinced that my tubing had rotted out forever. To piss meant contracting my abdomen as if giving birth. Even then, forcing and shaking, I could only squeeze out a broken, painful stream. I dreamed of pissing with the power of a fire hose. Of writing a full uninterrupted sentence of urine, a paragraph . . . maybe even a page or two. Instead I wrung out strange half-sentences filled with ellipses . . . a broken series of dots and dashes.

My father had his first experience with cancer five years before I got sick. Bladder cancer. Cancer has brought us together. We banter about our illnesses in a chummy, locker-room sort of way.

There is an unfortunate cliché about cancer victims: they are repressed, holding things in, too controlled. Despite our occasional pagan releases, my father and I fit this stereotype. I'm as driven with writing as he is building and selling textile machinery.

I cut out of the marsh and hike to the road. I head home, this time walking right down the middle of the street. I'm no longer afraid of seeing my neighbors—far from it, I propel myself with long strides. Feeling stronger by the minute, like a big cat on the prowl, I'm sure I could be hit by a car with no ill effects.

Back at the house, I drink beer as if it were water. I open a can, turn it upside down, and pour the contents straight into my stomach. No gulping involved, simply emptying the liquid as if into a vat. The beer tastes good—it slows me down, makes me calmer. I lie back in a lawn chair on the back deck and watch the slow show of clouds. "I prefer the natural sky to an opium-eater's heaven," said Thoreau. Not me. Not now.

I think about how a mushroom trip's arc mirrors the arc of life. At first nothing connects or makes sense, just colors and noises and sensations. It's all random images and no words—delight and fear. Then words return with a period of anxiety, the shifting moods of adolescence. Next confidence and power, followed finally by a deep, tired calm.

Looking down from above the marsh now, I imagine the bustling shipyard 140 years ago, when Thoreau walked through Suet. I see piles of white oak, not from the Cape's own dwarf trees, but brought in by train from Maine and western Massachusetts. I watch workers strip the trees of bark, steep the wood in hot water, stack it in the sun to dry. I see them steam and bow the planks in ovens to form the curving hull of the ship.

The whole scene looks a bit like a modern construction site, but there are differences. The ship is built on an enormous platform. Its massive frame takes shape like a rib cage. A derrick lowers the timbers of the ship's keel; the huge ribs are bolted into the keel's backbone. Holes are bored into the side; men caulk, tar, pound mallets. Finally, after months of effort, comes the releasing of the keel blocks. The ship creaks and slides down the hill into the sea.

The ships disappear. I stand up and walk to the edge of the deck. I take a leak into the brambles and watch the silver play in my broken stream. It feels wonderful and strange to pass water, as if my insides are gently running out of me. I feel older than I did an hour ago. My father is not the marsh. That was a foolish thought. My father is the shipyard *and* the marsh. Above, the upward building and frenetic energy; below, the murk, undefined, without boundaries, strange. He spends half his life building upward, the other half following some primitive impulse to undermine what he builds.

In this time of isms and support groups and victims, I'm sure that most people would argue that my father's wildness has less to do with any natural predisposition to disorder than with the vodka-and-tonic round which his hairy hand is often wrapped.

But it's more than drink. It's a delight in things feral and crude. In allowing wildness to undermine virtues.

Or is wildness the virtue? Doesn't each of us need to build up our lives, while remembering that we're always building on marshland? If we forget, there's a danger. A danger like the one we face when we fill in the "useless" marshes. We try to push the wild down, but it finds a way to break up through the grid. By destroying the marshes we destroy the world's stinkhorn. Its rank, creative place.

PAINTING CAPE COD

✣

Another storm is coming, a northeaster. As I walk out on
the jetty the waves swell up, trying to buffet me into the
sea. I stand at the end of the jutting rocks and watch a
chocolate-colored Wilson's petrel skim and skip above the water
like a well-thrown rock. At times it disappears, looks as if it's lost
forever inside a wave, but rises up again. Nearby terns fish. They
hover, then dive down sharply into the surf.

It's a drizzly cold day that does its best to strip the branches of
their leaves. The ocean is gray and frothy. During the night it
tossed quite a bounty onto the shore. In the first hundred yards of
my walk, I find a white plastic jug, a truck tire, a waterlogged life
jacket snagged on a rock, several beer cans made generic by the
waves, a yellow margarine tub, a rusted tripod, twine, Styrofoam,
and a small motor-oil container. Strewn through the sea's yard
sale are the gray and white feathers of a gull—the tide, apparently,
had battered the bird, then slunk away with its corpse—also, the
remains of two horseshoe crabs, turned on their backs, their
shells collecting rainwater.

The rain has cleared the beach of people, but I'm not alone. Behind the bluff I hear the crows. They seem to like the mizzling
weather. This morning they woke me, and I've been stumbling
across them all day, sending them off cawing. As I walk farther
out past the houses to the bluff, plovers lift in ranks in front of
me, glide over the water, fly twenty feet ahead, settle, lift again.
Black double-crested cormorants and white gulls sit on sharp
rocks just offshore.

I, too, take a seat, my back to the water. On wet days the
gnarled purples, yellows, and olive greens of the bluff are most
vivid. A soggy drawing pad is hidden in my coat, and I take it out
and sketch the bluff for perhaps the hundredth time. Before beginning, pencil poised, my mind paints a satiric self-portrait—the
earnest artist staring nobly at nature—but I shake the picture off
and get to work.

My paintings of the bluff are scattered across the country.

They reside in our basement gathering mildew, in the attic of my old house in Boylston, and on a friend's walls in Los Angeles. In Colorado one was tacked above my bed to remind me where I felt most at home. My paintings are rough and amateurish, done only for pleasure. "A change is as good as a rest," said Winston Churchill, referring to his own attempts with the brush. This is true. Each painting is a small vacation.

A vacation from what? From writing and its rigors. This morning my sluggish mind wouldn't react to the whip of daily discipline. Words slogged sleepily in my head and even the pinch of caffeine couldn't excite them. Staring ahead blankly, I met the sad, wooden eyes of a pen-and-ink sketch above my desk. These were the eyes of Thoreau, or at least a thin-lined pencil sketch of Thoreau I'd torn from a book. I've grown to dislike the picture—it makes Thoreau look dry and brittle, a man without blood, a husk. This morning his eyes seemed vaguely judgmental, preacherly. I pushed away from the desk, grabbed my sketch pad, and headed out of the house, feeling like I'd escaped a truant officer.

I began to paint after seeing an exhibit featuring Vlaminck and Derain, the so-called Fauves, or "wild animals." According to the biographical sketch I read at the exhibit, Vlaminck "painted with fury, applying the tubes straight onto the canvas."

The biography described him:

Over six feet tall, weighing fifteen stone (about a hundred and eighty seven pounds), red-haired and overflowing with energy which he devoted to cycling, sculling at Argenteuil, wrestling with professionals in suburban circuses.

Vlaminck's combination of athleticism and artistry inspired me. Soon after seeing the exhibit, I began applying my own tubes straight onto the canvas, creating my own faux fauves. With painting I could romanticize the process—something I was long past with writing. While I liked brushing on the paint well enough, I *loved* stacking my materials in the corner of the house, cleaning the mud-colored brushes with turpentine, and snorting in the rich toxic smell that would stay on my hands and clothing for days. Even the names on the tubes thrilled: viridian, yellow ocher, burnt sienna.

My silly paintings hardly satisfy. Cape Cod is as unique in its way as the impressionistic landscapes of France, and it deserves a great interpreter. This land—famous for its light—has attracted thousands of artists, but I have yet to find any paintings that match the Cape Cod inside my head. The Cape I love is a Cape of color. The strange gripping purple of the cranberry bog in December. The gnarled gray-blue locusts, the summer-squash orange of pine needles sticking to a wet road. The darkly stained shingles after a storm, the abandoned homes at sunset with their rectangular windows of molten gold. The eastern red cedar turned blue by its berries, the white chest of a seagull corpse heaving up from the sand, even the beauty of shining golden plywood husks as a new house is erected. That's the Cape I want to frame and hang on my walls.

Sketching the bluff, I try to imagine which great painters of the past I'd like to have paint Cape Cod. Marsden Hartley comes to mind. His paintings of Maine and the Massachusetts north shore, with their thick black cartoon outlines of robotic lobsterman and plates of gleaming fish, are close to what I'm looking for. But they're too stiff. Maybe Kandinsky. Not the painter of the famous compositional abstracts, but the younger Kandinsky whose landscapes were simple children's colors corralled by thick black lines where rivers flowed in unreal question marks. Maybe. But even those paintings are not juicy enough.

The paintings I desire would have to possess an element of caricature. I understand that "caricature" is now a dirty word, but while both painters I've mentioned employed black cartoon outlines, it's not cartooning I want. I want the exaggerations of landscape—the bursting hills, the trees and vines crawling up buildings, the fields aflame with unreal light. I want Jawlensky's faces, not Klee's anorexic cave paintings, which seemed scratched out by some dainty troglodyte. Excess. There is something of it in the paintings of Kirchner, Jawlensky, Munter, and, of course, Vlaminck and Derain.

But if I were allowed to choose only one painter, I would take a short step back in time and pick Vlaminck and Derain's spiritual father. I'd choose Vincent van Gogh to paint Cape Cod.

Not van Gogh, you say. *Please.* We're tired of him, tired of calenders and Japanese bidding wars. Fair enough; the man *is* a pop-culture icon. But to abandon him due to his popularity? Wouldn't that be just as bad as deserting a man because he's unpopular? A friend is a friend.

Anyway, there are more pertinent questions. Such as, Is he qualified? It's true that most of his paintings were of inland seas, but his few seascapes are impressive. One late August I visited Saintes Marie de la Mar. I remember dried fish blood on the jetties, dull orange roofs seen from the beach. Two weeks later in Zurich I saw his sketch of the town, and it brought back the scene exactly and vividly. In the same museum, I learned the man could paint a fish. Studying van Gogh's trout, I took rough notes: "Silver of the scales—vivid. Table beneath it lumpish, thick with paint. Short dashing strokes . . . Silver short strokes coming rapidly down . . . Slashing. Green jug. Turbulence. Eyes of fish and stems of tomatoes actually some centimeters off paper. White-blue, black, and silver."

While these caveman gropings are hardly articulate, they help me understand what I like most about van Gogh's painting. He wasn't afraid to make a mark on the canvas. He let you know he'd been there.

Now I must confess a hidden agenda in nominating van Gogh as the Cape's painter laureate. The complaint I have with the paintings of the Cape I've seen is a complaint I have with recent art and literature in general. There's a smallness, an overrefinement. A prettiness. A lack of sprawl and scope.

I'm guilty of the opposite crime. At one time, in my megalomaniacal youth, I wanted to use words to paint a van Gogh of the Cape. It was a lofty, egotistical ambition. I hoped to write a novel where the main character was the irrational, exaggerated landscape, the wind and salt swirling round the houses and undersized trees. I'd read and admired the Cape naturalists John Hay, Robert Finch, and Henry Beston, and I wanted to emulate their various adventures in nature. But the Cape I saw and experienced was not a naturalist's Cape. There was nothing understated or scientific about it. The elements were heaped on, overdone, churning. It was a Cape of strange swirling winds that affected me even in sleep. A Cape where the weather played an almost mystical role.

For ten years I tried to capture these forces in fiction. And failed. And now I've come back to the Cape to write small personal essays, commentaries on nature and myself. But as I climb up the side of the bluff, the wind blows strong and cold, snapping my windbreaker, and old delusions puff up inside.

Nagged by persistent romanticism, I still have trouble seeing the Cape as it is. "Excess is preferable to deficiency." My college professor, Walter Jackson Bate, often quoted this line of Samuel Johnson's. In lectures he compared the worst of neoclassicism to a desert, the worst of romanticism to a fetid swamp. "I like neither but if forced to choose one, I'd take the swamp," he said.

Van Gogh, too, knew where he stood:

You must boldly exaggerate the effects either of harmony or discord which colours produce; exact drawing, exact colour, is not the essential thing because a reflection of reality in a mirror, if it could be caught, colour and all, would not be a picture at all, no better than a photograph.

Two lines later he added: "And I think I have more chance of success if I don't cramp myself by working on too small a scale."

To work on a large scale and exaggerate! The naturalists write beautifully about the Cape, but sometimes it feels they've claimed this land for their own, muscling out anyone who doesn't know the Latin name of a sumac or plover. But we're not all scientists, and we still must allow ourselves to occasionally see more than what's visible. I wonder if a spirit of excess could blow

through our present artistic and literary climate like a northeast wind clearing the air. I wonder if we could benefit from art that is nervously close to caricature—heaped on, thick, overdone.

Below, black and white patterned eiders, their necks pistachio stained, bob on the waves. From my perch on the bluff I watch gnarled scrub oaks strain against wind and sea. If van Gogh could twist his fruit trees and cypresses into life, how easily could he animate these? The clouds tear apart gently and, for a quick second, sun laves my face. The gray ocean greens.

The Mediterranean has the colours of mackerel—changeable, I mean. You don't always know if it is green or violet; you can't even say it's blue, because the next moment the changing light has taken on a tinge of rose color or grey. . . . Now that I have seen the sea here I am absolutely convinced of staying in the Midi, and of piling on, exaggerating the colour.

Piling on. I stifle a histrionic impulse to sprint back home and heap exaggerated sentences on the page. So much for modest essays.

"Excess *is* preferable to deficiency," I yell excitedly to the gulls.

~

Back at the house I'm calmer. And slightly embarrassed. I remind myself of why I'm here. Not for any grand romantic thrashing, nor to paint. I stuff my sketch pad below my desk and pick up a pen and notebook.

How do we create the excitement of excess while keeping our wits about us? How do we see more while still seeing with clear eyes and a reasonable mind?

As I ask these questions, I meet again the doleful gaze of Thoreau. I no longer feel like running from him. Perhaps the stolidness of that look, contrasted with the gyrating and ever-maddening faces of van Gogh's self-portraits, holds a clue for me. *Walden* is the most excessive of books, a book bursting with health and joy and the urge to sing about it, but what was it built from? Minutiae from the journals. A scientist's collection of observed realities. Years and years of specifics, small bricks collected day after day that would be used to build the illusion of compression and intensity.

And so I turn back to my notes and record the unexciting specifics of my walk—the crows and cans of motor oil and persistent wind. For me this year is about health, not madness, more about Thoreau's cabin than the rages and depressions of van Gogh's yellow house.

I lean back and remember my first visit to Walden Pond. I was a freshman in college. It was a rainy day and I had an exhilarating time, at one point chasing a duck down to the water, but I was disappointed by something I saw at the cabin site. A cairn of rocks was piled next to the spot where Thoreau's eight-by-ten house once stood.

What could be a more ridiculous tribute? I wondered. *A senseless group piling of rocks to celebrate our most renowned individualist. How idiotic.*

But today, at this moment at least, I'm of a different mind. Older now, I like cairns, and think that cairn-making isn't such a bad mission. To heap on the rocks. One by one. To pile on and pile up senselessly until there is sense.

CARPENTRY

✟

Afew years after graduating from college I began working
as a carpenter on Cape Cod. I'd gotten to know the Cape
during summers and during one glorified off-season, so
perhaps the effect of that winter was palliative. I saw a different
Cape. Cape Cod as Siberia. Empty, cold, hard.

I moved back in late fall. The house was a shadowy icebox
where doors creaked and mice scratched behind the walls and
pipes gurgled like underground streams. Salt spray clouded the
windows. Out back, the post oak, which had always been my favorite tree, was losing its waxy leaves. The branches were black
and skeletal, an old withered hand clawing at the sky. At the
beach the eelgrass was the color of wheat. I could see winter coming in every branch, blade, and leaf.

I've never felt so thoroughly alone as I did that winter. By day
I helped build houses from the ground up, but after work I
turned to another kind of building. Sitting on the living-room
couch, the wind outside blowing so hard it seemed we'd be
swept out to sea, the light of the fire flickering and shooting
shadows round the room, a blanket draping my shoulders, I surrounded myself with books and coffee cups and wrote a draft of
a novel. This was long before I discovered the joy of word pro-
cessing, and I wrote in longhand. Occasionally my hand would
tingle and go numb and I'd shake it hard, like a pen needing ink,
until I could use it again.

I worked for Gus, a sinewy, shriveled man with a bitter laugh.
He'd worked outside through a dozen winters, earning him, in his
mind, a badge of toughness and a right to inhumanity.

I was anxious to impress Gus and ran from project to project,
hoping that what I gave in hustle would make up for what I
lacked in skill. One of my first tasks was to rip apart an old wall
in the cellar of the house we were rebuilding. I tore at it with all
my might, ripping and pulling it down with a pry bar and slamming into it with a sledge. Clouds of dust enveloped me.

I was naive, of course, and it wasn't until break that I finally asked what the wall was made of.

Gus gave me a half-smile, and spoke matter-of-factly.

"Asbestos," he said.

It was my first hint of things to come. Often over the next weekends I'd drive up to Boston, and when I returned on Monday morning I'd feel as if, crossing the bridge, I was driving back into another century. On the Cape, working for Gus, survival was the watchword. You were fighting the elements. You expected to die by fifty.

I was a terrible carpenter. I worked at it for the better part of three years, but never really became more than an apprentice. In my defense I must say I worked under a handicap. While some boys are raised by fathers who teach them about cat's-paws and chalk lines from a young age, I grew up with a man who taught me that tools were to be feared and distrusted.

My father believed that boards and nails had to be wrestled,

slammed, ultimately *willed* together. He passed this belief on to
me. We were not handy, and it was a sad sight when we tried to
work together on the Cape house. We cursed and muttered to ourselves, peppering the air with "goddamn"s and "Jesus"s, our faces
growing beet red, our temples throbbing as we tried to fix old
screen doors or patch up the bulkhead. We fought an absurd and
endless fight. The house sagged and sunk back into the earth
while we, ineptly but determinedly, battled to boost it back up.

Survival was foremost in my mind the winter I worked for Gus.
My house was poorly heated and I slept in a sweatshirt and sweat-
pants that doubled as long underwear. I'd get out of my cold bed
and pull on my cold boots and work clothes, grab my tool belt and
run down to my car. After stopping at Cumberland Farms for coffee, I drove to the job site. Work began at seven-thirty sharp. My
first task each day was to unpack the van, the nail guns, tool-
boxes, and extension cords. I did this in a near sprint, hoping to
fight off the cold. It was a stormy winter and many mornings my
next job was sweeping the snow off the plywood floors. I worked
hard. For some unfathomable reason, it was important to me to
gain Gus's respect.

At night I wrote and dreamed of creating a swirling, violent
portrait of the Cape, a New England *Wuthering Heights*. But
there was nothing romantic about the work I did during the day. I
worried about frostbite. We wore gloves at work, but holes soon
appeared and spread across the fingers. I spent late November
mornings shooting nails into plywood. Once Gus walked up behind me as I was taking off my glove and blowing on the bare skin.

"You think this is cold, my friend," he laughed. "Just wait till
the real cold comes."

He picked up a long orange extension cord. The protective
coating on the cord had worn off in several places; some of the
spots were now covered with black electric tape, some still exposed. He waved the cord under my nose.

"You see this cord?" he asked. "Every once in a while you'll
pick it up on the wrong spot. Then you'll feel a shock run down
your arm and straight through your body."

He dropped the cord, spit.

"Well, my friend, there'll be days when you're going to want to grab right onto that cord. . . . You're going to want to grab it hard right on one of those places where the rubber's gone. You'll be up there on the roof wrestling with the rafters, feeling the frostbite on your hands and the wind blowing straight through you, and you'll want to grab hold. . . . You won't care about being electrocuted. You'll just want to get warm."

He cackled. Then he quoted an advertisement for Old Milwaukee beer that he was fond of repeating like a sarcastic mantra.

"It doesn't get any better than this," he said.

After work I drove home and took long walks by the water. By January the harbor was choked with ice. Floating blocks clogged it for some forty yards out. The ice was solid by the shore but broken up farther out. Around that time the neighbor's German shepherd drowned by straying out too far on the blocks. Water sloshed beneath the floes.

Ice covered the trees. Silver laced the branches of the post oak—they chattered and clicked, their reflection dancing a spidery dance over blue shadows of snow. At night I continued to write my novel in longhand. It was this moonlighting that finally did me in. Firing the nail gun for eight hours followed by scribbling sentences down in my notebooks proved too much. In early February I woke up one night at four in the morning. The thumb and first three fingers of my right hand tingled and throbbed. The next night there was no throbbing. No feeling at all. I walked around the frozen house shaking my hand furiously, but it wouldn't respond.

Through February the numbness continued, and once or twice the idea of grabbing hold of the old extension cord crossed my mind. I didn't have health insurance, so didn't visit a doctor. Having no idea what was wrong, I wrote melodramatic notes to myself, bemoaning my fate. "I can't write without my hand. I have to finish the book before I lose it. They will not take my hands from me!"

On top of Gus's other charming traits, he was an anti-Semite. One day at break we were sitting on top of a snowy pile of two-bysixes, turning our faces up toward the dull winter sun. The mason and electrician were taking break with us, and I watched Gus as he ate three Hostess crumb cakes, dunking them into the top of a blue thermos mug filled with steaming coffee. He spoke to us as he ate, displaying a mouthful of soggy, half-chewed pastry.

"What went wrong with my sister is simple," he told us. "First, she got pregnant. Second, she married a Jew."

He sighed and took another sip of coffee. He crumpled the cellophane wrapper that held his crumb cakes.

"Well, it ain't all bad. You should see the rock he gave her. I mean this guy was born with money. He doesn't just go get her a ring at a store. He calls up this guy he knows in the Jew section of New York. He gives the guy a list of what he's looking for in a ring.

"Well, you should see the thing he ends up giving her. The thing's the size of a fuckin' baseball. I was talking to him last month at a dinner party, and he thinks nothing of it. I mean this guy has never lived in the real world. He doesn't know what money is."

"Knows a lot more about it than you or I ever will," the electrician interjected.

They all laughed, and, I, sitting on the edge of the little circle, heard my own laughter join theirs. I hated myself for it, but hated Gus more. I studied his face. He was smiling his mean, leathery smile. His skin was deeply lined, and when he laughed the wrinkles balled up around his little eyes, burying them. The wrinkles were sharp, slicing lines, like paper cuts. They were even deeper when Gus squinted, and he was always squinting. Crow's feet on top of crow's feet, as if some insane bird had stomped on his face and, not content to strike once or twice, had danced a mad goosestep over his half-closed eyes.

"Welp," he said. "Back to work."

He smiled again as he pushed up and stood. Standing he still seemed bent over himself, with elbows and knees so sharp they looked like they might cleave through his skin. The skin itself was pulled taut over the bones and joints—canvas over tent posts. His teeth were yellow and chipped: they slanted backward toward his throat so that it was a wonder he could close his mouth without cutting himself. This, combined with the upward and outward point of his nose, gave him an openly aggressive look like an attacking ferret or weasel.

Finally, in March, I shelled out the money and went to see a doctor. I learned I had carpal-tunnel syndrome. A swelling in my forearm was pressing the small circle of bones in my wrist against the medial nerve, numbing all but my pinkie and part of my fourth finger. My hand would just keep getting worse unless I stopped using it, or got an operation, which I couldn't afford.

I had a perfectly legitimate reason to quit. But the thought of telling Gus terrified me. I drove out to the job site in Brewster and muttered my medical excuse, sure he didn't believe a word of it. Standing in front of him I felt worthless, a little college-boy who couldn't cut it.

Ten minutes later all was different. Driving back to East Dennis in my car, I hooted and sang, feeling as free as I've ever felt. I had escaped.

I couldn't survive a single winter as a Cape carpenter.

I didn't like Gus, but he taught me something about Cape Cod. About the grittiness and determination needed long after the summer people leave.

The Cape may not be a true island, but certainly men like Gus are true islanders. For him, the Cape might as well be Alcatraz, Boston might as well be a million miles away. Locals call the world over the bridge "Off-Cape," defining it by what it's not. As a geographical region, Off-Cape includes Thailand as well as Duxbury.

Despite his bitterness and bigotry, I admire Gus. I think of him as an organic extension of Cape Cod. As it is for the pitch pines that grow on the dunes above Stone's bluff, life for him is a daily fight against cold and wind and water. The chest-high pines cling to the top of the sandy rise, bending backward away from the sea, their prickly needles growing only on the shore side. Like Gus, these trees seem to have struck a deal with the Cape and its elements. The deal requires giving up any grandeur, beauty, or height, anything lofty or extravagant. And what do they, Gus and the trees, get in return for this grudging and shriveled life, for days and years of fighting against the wind and cold? Not much. Not much or, depending on how you look at it, everything. They are granted just one thing and that is the right to survive.

I went back to carpentry a few years later. My hand felt better and I needed the money.

My new boss was a small man with nugget brown eyes and a black pageboy haircut, who looked a little like the singer Paul Simon. His name was Carl Hogan. The first thing that impressed me about Carl was the way he moved, slowly, casually, calmly, and at times lazily, as if underwater. He spoke in a steady quiet voice, almost a whisper, and if I was too concerned about doing something perfectly, he'd try to relax me.

"Remember," he'd say. "We're building a house, not a piano."

Carl ambled from one project to another while things—decks, beams, walls—mysteriously sprouted up around him. He sipped tea while he worked, and at first I thought this held the key to his character. I was a coffee fanatic and considered those who didn't drink it somehow unmanly.

"He's a *tea drinker*," I sneered in my journal.

But while his choice of beverage offended me, his calm dazzled. On one of our first days together we built a deck. Carl moved in a slow, almost sleepy manner, ambling over to a stack of pressure-treated lumber the color of unripe bananas. He cut the wood to length, hooking his tape measure over one end of a board, then walking down to the other, marking the distance with his flat, short pencil, and drawing a line across with the help of the try square. I ran to assist him like an overanxious nurse, but he seemed to think it was enough for me to just watch.

He pinned the boards on his knee with one hand and picked up his power saw with the other. One by one, he lopped off the ends of the boards. When the last was cut, he hefted it up on his shoulder and walked back to the deck. There he dropped to one knee and rolled it down his arm. He adjusted the board and hammered it into place. Three sixteen-penny nails per joist. *Pound, pound, pound.* Even the way he hammered was casual—almost slow—but he hit the nail heads cleanly. The long Estwing framing hammer looked like a sledge in his small hand. When he brought it down the wood squirted and the nail disappeared. One nail after another—*pound, pound, pound*—and then, the last nail sunk, he ambled back to the green pile to retrieve the next piece.

To me, there was something magical about the way he worked. Unhurried, but efficient. Most of the time it looked as if he wasn't hustling nearly enough, and if my father had been watching, he would have been driven insane. "Where is the bustling?" he would have wondered. "The *drive*? The *fury*?"

Even more perplexing was the mystery of how Carl finished things so quickly. Despite his idling, wood and nails grew from the back of the house. After the first day, four huge posts had branched out of the patio, and two-by-eights budded on top of the posts. Soon after—the second day? the third?—we were staring at a magnificent creation, a deck that cantilevered up and out over the surrounding trees and bushes. There was no logical explanation, and when I asked him to explain he mumbled something about "not wasting motion." I knew it couldn't be that simple. The answer was something stranger, more mystical.

Later I heard criticism of Carl from my workmates. They said he didn't finish jobs, didn't bid high enough, didn't pay bills, didn't settle squabbles between employees. Some of this was mere hearsay, but if he was flawless as a craftsman, he was less so as an administrator. His faults were the opposite of mine and my father's. He was *too* relaxed.

But, for me, Carl was a revelation. On some level I had always believed that for work to be great it must somehow be obsessive, intense, crazy. I even used the phrase, "I'm going to go crazy," when entering a particularly productive phase. My college heroes had been Dostoyevsky and van Gogh, and deep down I believed that, to accomplish anything in this world, you had to whip yourself into a froth of intensity.

But here was a new hero. A calm, reasonable man. I tried so hard to be more like Carl, to change my life and uproot the romantic weeds. To become more modest, honest, simple. To become, against all odds, a reasonable man myself.

Remarkably, I'd never learned to use a power saw while working for Gus. For the most part I'd spent my time toting equipment and boards, and nailing wood together with the gun. Now Carl took time out to teach me how to use a saw.

In a calm voice, he broke the procedure down. He extended his tape measure to the end of a board with a shuffling motion, then marked the correct spot with a pencil and drew a straight line with his try square. Next, he jammed the wood down in the nook formed by his shin and foot, and, moving the saw steadily through the board, sliced off the last six inches.

I nodded, but waited until he was gone to try it myself. If I was going to fail at something so simple, I would at least fail in private. I stared down at the pile of wood and tools. I picked up the cold metal handle of the saw, then put it down instantly. Fumbling nervously with the tape measure, I drew a trembling line at the prescribed fifty-two inches.

I picked up the saw for the second time and pulled the trigger. The blade whirled and blazed, dozens of jagged shark's teeth only inches from my leg. Trying not to think, I pinned the board as Carl had shown me and moved the teeth toward the wood. When the saw hit, it began to jag out a line like an excited patient's heartbeat on a cardiograph. After two or three seconds, it jammed completely. I tried to force the blade forward, but it wouldn't move—the teeth froze in midbite. Panicked, I reared back and gave the saw a good hard push, putting all my weight behind it.

The impossible happened. The saw, seemingly of its own will, pounced back toward my face. It came flying, arcing toward me, its teeth blazing round and round in a wild whirl. I screamed "Fuck!" fell to the ground, and scuttled backward like a crab, the crazed teeth suspended above me in the air. I lay there, unable to move, sure that the saw would slice me in half. Finally, after an interminable slow-motion arc, the blade touched down an inch from my foot. It bit into the ground, spun, chewed up dirt, sputtered and died.

"Fuck," I said again, whispering this time. I lay there, my heart pounding like a jackhammer, as Carl rounded the corner.

I tried to explain what had happened while he looked down at me, his expression patient, and a little amused.

"It must have bound up on you," he said simply, and walked away.

Bound up. Maybe. But I knew what I knew. The saw had tried to kill me.

While he worked, Carl wrote down ideas on a shingle with his stubby carpenter's pencil. They were casual and quickly drawn plans for what was to be built that day or over the next week. Once I took one of these discarded shingles home with me, studying the notes like hieroglyphs.

I have always overplotted. Both my own life and my fiction. Trying to control how things will be, I make outlines and charts of how mine and my character's lives *should* go. I print out lists and outlines and staple them together. Not allowing for natural growth, I try to predetermine events, and, if they don't follow my orders, I become angry and frustrated.

What a relief to think life could be organized quickly and casually on the back of a shingle.

Once, in late September, I spent a few weeks shingling the roof of Carl's own house. It was a beautiful fall, filled with good cold winds and crusty leaves that scraped along the streets. We spent entire days up on the roof, unwrapping peanut butter and jellies during lunch, smelling the sawdust, staring out at the bay.

The house was a tall and ungainly saltbox, and we worked on thin staging supported by roof brackets nailed in a bit too casually by Carl. I enjoyed the work despite fearing occasionally that I'd fall to my death.

Carl rented out two thirds of the house. The renters claimed the front doors, and to get into Carl's apartment you had to walk up an outside stairway with several of the treads missing, several more covered only with unnailed planks. At the top of the stairs you entered by climbing through a hole cut in the wall. Everything about the apartment was makeshift and half-built. A woodstove sat in the middle of the living room. The bathroom door was not on its hinges, but stood against the wall next to the bathroom. If you needed privacy you simply picked up the door and leaned it over the entrance. The place was filled with hidden nooks. High on the wall above the stove, bricks had been knocked out to tunnel into a room in another section of the house. A ladder led up to the hole.

I was charmed by many things about the house, but the two-by-four walls impressed me most. Carl had never sheetrocked them, so the skeletal beams were not really walls, but clear for all to see. Maybe this was pretension, to act so unpretentious, but at the time it seemed to me a wonderful new way to live. Unadorned, simple, without exterior show or sham.

This morning the ocean looks olive green by shore, Bermuda aquamarine further out, and further still quite literally a deep blue. An older man in a yellow slicker clams on the flats, his movements patient and sure.

I've been working, too. Earlier I cleaned out the cellar, watching the green of the pines through the bulkhead. A beam of light shone in and dust particles danced within the beam. I shoveled out a pile of coal dust. The shovel bit into the dirt with a hard chomping sound. My arms felt good, chomping in, swinging. Repeating the motion over and over. Next I tore up and rebuilt a couple of steps on the back deck, then built a plywood garbage bin to keep the dogs and raccoons out of the trash. This afternoon I might reshingle a small part of the east wall.

It's nice to have these skills. While I work I imitate Carl's relaxed shuffle, not my father's frantic charge.

I also feel Carl's influence as I build this book. I'm tired of fiction. Tired of inventing. Particularly tired of the tendency that invented characters have of possessing you, of holding on to you for years. Fiction is compulsion, danger. With fiction you must get up each day and attack—an onward military march like working for Gus. There isn't time to think or doubt. You work in a near frenzy, and if you slow down, the cold gets you. I turn to nonfiction for relief.

These days I take long walks by the ocean and scribble down the beginnings of essays. I wander, keep things rambling, half-completed. I try not to overplot. If I had a shingle, I'd sketch plans on it. Sometimes it feels these pieces are growing on their own, sprouting up around me. Melville called the state I'm in a "grass growing mood."

We do people a disservice when we make them into symbols. We use primary colors, ignore their complexity or pain. Still, this morning I think of Carl and the walls of his house. For years I tried to erect grand structures, but not this winter. I keep my sentences simple and unadorned. I try to speak in a voice with the beams showing, tell the truth with simple planks. Of course, it's as easy to romanticize simplicity as anything else, but for the moment I write with Carl Hogan in mind.

I also try not to forget that, despite what I grew up learning, there *is* room for error.

"Remember," I hear Carl say. "You're building a house, not a piano."

KILLING FATHERS

✛

The news is my father has cancer.
Not like last time, when the toilet bowl was bright pink with blood, and it attacked his bladder. Not like last time when it was a "controllable" type of cancer.

This time it is bad.

It starts with a message from my mother on the machine: "David, we just got back from the doctor's. I need to talk to you as soon as possible."

I take notes as she tells me the news. "Malignant carcinoma," I scribble down. She tells me my father will call me later.

I don't cry or even feel particularly sad at first. I'm a step or two removed, at the same time guilty for feeling so removed. Then I get angry. I storm around the house, my father's house. I slam my fist up into the chocolate beams. Sawdust falls from the beetle holes like snow. "Goddamn it," I yell at the phone. "Come on you fucker—*ring.*"

I recognize this reaction to trouble. Getting angry. It's the way my father reacts.

But when I finally talk to him he isn't angry. He sounds like he does when he's doing what he's so often doing, taking care of the rest of us. He focuses on the practical. Getting things "organized."

"These things happen," he says. "We'll find out what's going on and we'll take it from there. I've got to put a lot of things in order over the next month. I've got to get us organized."

I listen to the familiar, habitual phrase. "Getting organized," was repeated like a mantra in our house. The words no longer bother me, not the way they once did.

Most of the anger I felt toward my father during my teens and twenties is gone.

Not long ago I had a dream in which I was gently stroking his bald head.

I stay up late, feeding the wood stove. I use the hook to remove the circular cover and stare into the burning belly. The stove, a squat, iron god, dominates the living room and requires constant sacrifices. Not long ago I thought I'd gathered an inexhaustible supply of wood—kindling piled high in the old crib by the fireplace, two cords of oak stacked against the house, and piles of unused ends, discarded pieces of two-by-fours and two-by-tens, broken shingles. This I supplemented with daily beach walks to gather driftwood.

Now, inexplicably, the wood is almost gone. The bin empty, I charge out of the house, letting the storm door slam shut behind me. I run through the hard snow; the pebbly grains climb up over my hightop sneakers and melt against my ankles. I crunch over to the old picnic table and flip it on its back, like a rodeo cowboy downing a steer. It lies there, its two remaining legs straight up in the air. There is little wood left on it; it's like a well-picked turkey carcass a week after Thanksgiving. I saw frantically at the remaining legs, using the rusted-out Stanley saw with the head like an owl. I saw maniacally, swearing at myself, freezing, ready to quit. It's too cold. I cut the legs halfway through, and then kick. The pieces break off unevenly and, when the last piece cracks and falls, I gather the pile to my chest. I run back through the crusty snow.

Once I jam the wood deep into the stove, the flames begin to jump. I keep my purple hands right above the flames. I stand there, up to my wrists in the stove. I shake my fingers over the fire. My hands tingle as the blood rushes back.

"Thank God you didn't get your novel published."

This the reaction of my ex-girlfriend, a doctor now, when I tell her my father is sick.

The novel is called *Wormtown*. I based it on my own experience with testicular cancer, and the relationship between a father and son is at the book's heart. I've been pushing furiously to get *Wormtown* published.

Suddenly being published doesn't seem so important. I agree with her. Thank God.

Rereading some of the lines from the book I cringe. The portrait of my father is raw caricature. Bulging eyes. Toad-like features. Fat stomach. In real life my father is a powerful, compassionate man with a strong way of being in the world. In the novel he's heavier, crueler, and more irrational. Out of curiosity I killed off my mother early in the second chapter. I wondered just how much living alone would affect the character based on my father. As it turned out it made him drink and made him mean.

"The first ten years of a writer's career are a catharsis of resentment," wrote Auden. *Wormtown* was an angry book. Why was I angry? I was angry because I hadn't become the success my father was. Angry because he hadn't given me the support I felt I needed to become that success. Angry because I had cancer.

Growing up I always admired my father's sense of humor. His bluntness. The way he'd cut through the circumlocution of others with his favorite phrase—"No more bullshit." Also the way he poked fun at friends, though "poked" hardly does justice to his semisadistic stabbings.

I listened with delight to his attacks. And I learned well at the feet of the master. In my novel I took my father's weapons and turned them against him.

A few months ago, before I learned my father was sick again, I rationalized my decision to push the book despite the pain it might cause him. Like most people who do these sorts of things, I justified my decision in the name of art. I wrote:

> My art is confessional. My father is a private man, but I, on paper and in person, like to blurt things out.
>
> I am a father-killer. While the last thing I want to do is cause him pain, the book dies without the conflict between father and son. I think the exaggerated descriptions of the senior Brunner are the best things I've ever done.
>
> I've spent two years of my life on this novel. I suppose one thing I could, and do, half-hope for, is to not be published. But if I ever do get it published, I know in my heart I'll follow through. I'll plunge in the knife. I won't change a word.

Tough words. And untrue. It's the novel, not my father, that I now kill. It's resting place is a dusty drawer behind my filing cabinet. Two years of my life shelved. R.I.P.

Is there any place on earth as empty as the Cape in winter? Nothingness. A pale barren land that imagination can't fill. The brambles and bushes are empty; you can see straight through to the

harbor. An occasional purple stem twists among the pale white. The beach grass is like wheat in a drought, the sand colorless and vast. I walk by the water and stare out; it looks green and sickly, and remarkably still. I'm struck by the lack of sound: no birds, no wind, not even the waves lapping as they do on the calmest of days. The absence of everything.

Later the wind returns, blowing life back across the bay. Curling bruised clouds reflect in the mud puddle behind the harbor dumpster. At the marsh I stumble upon a dead raccoon. At first I nearly miss it, the fur camouflaged by the beige surroundings. The corpse rests in a bed of salt-meadow cord grass, encircled by reeds that swirl round it. It looks to be a comfortable grave. A good grave.

I've always sought out fathers. I'm obsessed with them. Thoreau went to the woods to live deliberately; I went to the woods because Thoreau did. I comb biographies for personal details. Details that can, in the words of Samuel Johnson, "be put to use." I search for the secret of how to live. How to write.

What is this if not a search for a father who can teach me how to be?

How did some of the authors I admire—my literary fathers—treat *their* fathers in their fiction? Philip Roth's fictional father in *Portnoy's Complaint* was constipated and ineffectual, a Jewish joke held up for all to see. While Roth's fictional mother had magical powers and could "accomplish anything," the father was a laxative-chewing, self-annihilating drudge.

How did Roth's real father react to this portrayal? Judging from Roth's post-Portnoy fiction, the answer is "not very well." In *Zuckerman Unbound*, Roth's protagonist, Nathan Zuckerman, writes a book called *Carnovsky*, which like *Portnoy's Complaint*, scandalizes the writer's family. Later in life Zuckerman torments himself over having killed his father and alienated his brother with his writing.

This is how the drama proceeds in Roth's fictional world. But not, apparently, how it proceeded in life. Roth has written that in actuality his father was fiercely proud of, and defensive about, his work. And while Zuckerman tells himself to *"Forget fathers,"* Roth himself did quite the opposite. In *Patrimony*, Roth's nonfictional description of his father's illness and death, he looks at his father, his real father, with clear eyes. He writes:

> "I must remember accurately," I told myself, "remember everything accurately so that when he is gone I can recreate the father who created me."

My dreams of my father have not always been tender ones. I remember grabbing the thin red tufts of hair above his ears and banging his head to the ground while yelling *"Fuck, fuck, fuck you"* into his face.

Then there's Thomas Wolfe. He stood six foot seven, and among father killers was a true giant. "You have crucified your family and devastated mine," a friend wrote after the publication of *Look Homeward Angel*. After reading the same book, his brother responded; "On the impulse of the moment, I could have committed murder."

Wolfe saved the worst for Dad. He turned his father into a thumb-licking, alcoholic lecher who charged about with jerky cartoon movements, a paragon of wildness and pettiness and excess. And Wolfe not only fought dirty, he fought against a corpse.

Wolfe's mother, Julia, wrote of her husband that had he been "there to fight for the living it would be all right. But the dead have no comeback."

Wolfe reacted to this and other hometown criticism by invoking the good old goddess of art. "No matter what Asheville thinks now, they will understand in time that I tried to write a moving honest book about great people," he said. But how much of this art was a "catharsis of resentment"? The colossal Wolfe raged against the small people of Asheville: "They hate me. They're so damned little they smell little." The question that begs to be asked is, Who really was the little one? His recent biographer, David Donald, writes that Wolfe could never admit to himself how much of "writing his novel had been a way of purging himself of his bitterness toward members of his own family and repaying old social snubs."

I just returned from a week in North Carolina visiting my family. My father picked me up at the airport and drove me right to the Charlotte Coliseum to watch the Hornets play. This was appropriate. Sports have always been one way we communicate easily and well. Though he walked with a cane and had lost twenty pounds, he was still my father. He gloated over his car's new handicapped sticker, which allowed him to park right in front of the Coliseum.

"There are some advantages to having cancer," he brayed.

He was tired and in pain during the game, but still managed to complain about the cheerleaders, about people who bring babies to games, about the management calling the coliseum "The Hive."

"Bees have hives," he grumbled. "Hornets have *nests*."

The game was a thriller. With Charlotte down by eight with three minutes left, Mugsy Bogues began to steal every ball in sight. The Hornets rallied to win. During those last minutes everyone in the place was standing. Except my father. Unable to lift himself, he tried to peek out at the court through a forest of limbs.

"I'm glad I got to see one last game," he told me as I helped him to the car.

~

Once others began attacking *Look Homeward Angel,* Julia Wolfe reacted as any mother would. Donald describes her defiant attitude. She was hurt by her son's book, but she was also proud of him. "He's the only Asheville author who ever sold 100,000 copies," she bragged.

Who can say that W. O. Wolfe, Thomas's father, wouldn't have bragged right along with her? While alive, he positively gloated over his son's writing. "He had his soul wrapped up in you and what he thought you would one day be," wrote Julia. His sister added: "You know how Papa always wanted us to succeed, and how he always said, 'Don't be a nonentity.'"

Wolfe listened to his Dad. He wasn't a nonentity. And his father, or at least a warped portrait of his father, still survives today.

I wonder. How much of the elder Roth's pride in his son came from the writing's tremendous success? The ordinary pride of a father for a son who done good.

Which is the worse crime? Killing the father? Or failing by not killing him brilliantly?

The week in the South was difficult. My father's pain was so severe he could barely move, but still he kept his grace, his humor, his toughness. And his voice. It's a gruff businessman's voice that's been branded in my head since childhood. He talked about "fighting this goddamn war till the end."

"I've put a lot of things to bed in the last week," he said. "I'm almost organized."

And: "No sense moaning and groaning. You've got to play the cards they deal you."

During the middle of the week we drove up to Duke Medical Center and met Doctor Moore, who would be coordinating treatment. "My quarterback," my father called him. His strongest pain pills he called "bombers." He began chemotherapy—"blasting the bad guys"—and when he became nauseous told us, "it isn't all fun and games here at big kid's cancer camp."

I scribbled down and recorded his words. My father's voice rings as distinctly and powerfully in my ears as the Old Testament

God's. On the plane home I wondered: is it any surprise that it's taken me so long to develop a voice of my own? How can I have my own voice when all I hear is his?

They say we must kill our heroes to stand on our own. But I will always be a hero worshiper, will always look for others to teach me how to be. Part of accepting myself is accepting that I'll always search for fathers. I think of Montaigne, sitting in his attic room, the quotes from his literary heroes inscribed on the beams. Part of what made his voice unique was his acceptance that he leaned heavily on predecessors.

The traditional wisdom is that when a parent dies, the oldest same-sex child becomes more and more like that parent. Maybe so. Maybe I'll grow more gruff and businesslike. Or maybe, with my father gone, my voice will become more and more my own.

Theorizing aside, I know one thing. I will write about my father with respect, even if my "art" suffers for it. His portrait will not be a caricature, will not be cruel. And I know this. While he now leans on me, I could do worse than to lean on my father.

After a week away, my body is back on Cape Cod, but my mind stays behind in North Carolina.

I get up early and set to resurrecting the wood stove. I'm afraid I'll find it cold, but the charred embers are still glowing with tints of red. I simply open the vents and the fire jumps to life. I add a split log and shreds of newspaper. Amazing how a fire, like a man, can sleep, expending the least possible energy, then rise again. Throughout the night the vents were cracked only slightly, just enough oxygen to keep it alive. As I open them wide, the stove breathes heavily. It sucks in air and fills the room with its heat.

I remember how I felt about the wood stove when I first tried to live here alone years ago. What could be more dangerous and crazy, I wondered, than having a box of fire sitting in the middle of the living room? It seemed an infernal black demon that demanded worship through care and feeding. There wasn't a day that passed without my thinking about how easily its flames could catch on a curtain or blanket and start the house burning. Just one great belch and my father's house would burn to the ground.

Now I stare off the back deck and wonder if he'll ever return here. I head inside the empty house. Solitude is good for some things. For rumination and writing, for instance. But it isn't very good for worry. Or depression. Or hypochondria.

Three nights after I return I feel the lump on my neck. It is large and full. It could be nothing, I tell myself. Or it could be the end.

I sleep poorly. The next morning I drive to Cape Cod Hospital. The first doctor doesn't know what to make of my "tumor." The second diagnoses it as shingles. The lump is merely my lymph node, swollen and made hard by a virus.

Shingles, mumps, syphilis, they can call it what they will. I'll call it a sympathetic illness. If he has bumps on his skin, I'll have them, too. We are forever intertwined.

THE USES OF OUTRAGE

✣

I sit in the attic of the Cape house reading the newspaper and thinking about cancer rates on the Upper Cape. They're climbing again. Percentages and statistics float by my eyes. "39 percent above average for Upper Cape in 1988. . . . Women in Falmouth 79% more likely to contract cancer. . . . Moderate increases in brain cancer in Barnstable and Falmouth."

Seeing "moderate" in the same sentence with "brain cancer" gives me a start. Until now I've read these statistics without any emotional connection. Just words—they seem weightless, feathery, too light really to touch my life. I've been reading them with the distance I read about people starving in Africa, though Falmouth is significantly closer than Ethiopia. Now I remind myself that each one of the listed cases is a human being.

The word "apathetic" is bandied about quite a bit in describing Americans. But "numb" works better. Every day we read about outrageous crimes and deaths, and nod as if in a trance. Wouldn't it be healthier if, just once, we thundered righteously? If we threw the paper down and stormed about the house kicking over footrests and books?

After breakfast I drive down Route 6, past the familiar stunted pines and leafless oak, back to Hyannis. I walk through the front door of the Cape Cod *Times*, just as I did ten years ago when I worked as their cartoonist. Then I shook with fear that my cartoons would be rejected. But today I'm not nervous. I'm here to use the library.

The librarian is helpful. I thumb through the files, trying to make sense of a pile of statistics. I jot down facts. From 1982 through 1990 the cancer rate on the Upper Cape was about 25 percent above the state average. The raw numbers were actually higher, but the region's elderly population had to be factored in, lowering the percentage. Disturbingly, the percentage was worse in the most recent study, 1990—42 percent above the state average. Women were by far the hardest hit. Joel Feigenbaum, a Cape

Cod Community College math professor and official Cape cancer gadfly, says:

> In disease after disease, in town after town, we keep seeing this elevation in women. I would defy anyone in public health to find any place in the nation where anyone has ever seen this kind of profile of female elevations.

The rising rates are a mystery. Boston University was commissioned to do a half-million-dollar study in an attempt to determine the cause. It released the report in January 1992, concluding that environmental factors had little to do with the problem. But many are skeptical, Joel Feigenbaum among them. Along with the myriad of environmental threats, he points out that the rates began going through the roof twenty years after the local military base began its buildup for the Vietnam War.

Even the authors of the study admit their conclusions aren't final and urge more work in exploring the connection between environment and cancer on Cape Cod. "If someone wants to do continued research, there's lots to do," says one of the authors, David Ozonoff. "What we did was plant some signs that say, 'Dig here.'"

Meanwhile, the rates themselves remain a puzzle, and people remain fearful and uncertain. Only one clear fact exists: if you live on the Upper Cape you are more likely to get cancer than if you don't live there.

1983: I stare down at the great greased skull of Mengelthorpe, the Cape Cod Times *editor, while he, in turn, stares at my work. I await his verdict.*

"One thing that bothers me quite a bit," he says finally, "is that your cartoons always seem to be rather, well, mean-spirited."

My heart sinks.

"It seems you're always looking on the negative side of things. I don't see why you must constantly poke fun. What we're looking for—what we want from you—is something more positive, more upbeat. Your work is too crude and mean. You've got to understand that it's possible to draw positive cartoons."

I stare ahead like a zombie. He licks his thumb and turns the pages of the Boston Globe, *scanning the newsprint.*

"You see there are a lot of upbeat state and local issues out there," he continues, "Look . . . look at this one. Now here's an article about a blind sailor from Somerville. He's going to try and cross the Atlantic in a sailboat all by himself! Now that's rather heroic, isn't it? Certainly, you could do something positive about that."

That night I can't sleep. I stay awake thinking about Mengelthorpe and his blind sailor. I'm dealing with a man who wants upbeat cartoons. "Positive" cartoons. Was Herblock ever asked by his editors to do something "positive" about Nixon? Did George Grosz draw "upbeat" cartoons about Hitler?

We live on a beautiful peninsula that's being gobbled up daily by money-hungry developers. The Cape is being destroyed. We have a clear fight on our hands. Good versus bad. Black hats versus white.

The target is out there and I've tried to hit it. I've tried to do my job as a political cartoonist. But do they want me to fight the Cape's evils? No. They want me to draw a "positive" cartoon about a blind sailor. They want cartoons about seagulls and dump stickers and town meetings. They want a cheerleader when what they need is an attack dog. I have a battle on my hands worthy of Thomas Nast's struggle against Tammany Hall, but they want me to fight it with a pillow. Actually, they don't want me to fight it at all. They want me to award cartoons like citizen's medals for good behavior.

I drive home with a packet full of cancer articles in my lap. Pulling into the gravel driveway, I stare up the hill, knowing the house will soon be diminished for me.

Why am I here? I don't mean this existentially, but specifically why *here.* Why aren't I out West getting on with my life? Why not in North Carolina taking care of my father?

Ten minutes later I settle down on the back deck with a beer and read: "In 1990, 704 people living on the Upper Cape were diagnosed with cancer—about 200 more than would have been expected based on the state average for that disease."

Absorbing this information, something healthy happens. I get pissed off. I run upstairs to my writing desk and begin an angry letter to the Cape Cod *Times*.

I ask how anyone can be so idiotic as to think that environmental problems haven't affected the Cape's cancer rate. We've been contaminating this soil since the first encounter. A list of the environmental threats reads like a litany of plagues: the pesticides applied aerially to the cranberry bogs, the chemicals in Johns pond, the propellant bag burning at the military base, the PCE from the pipes used to transport town water, the firing of artillery guns and the storage of rocket fuel (a probable cause of colon cancer), the sewage dumped in our oceans, and the nuclear power plant sitting on the other side of the bridge.

"Your cartoons don't have any charm," Mengelthorpe tells me another time. "You have to try and make them more appealing."

He pauses to slide his hand over his greased hair.

"You know, ap-PEEL-ing," he says. "Like a banana." He smiles.

Ha, ha, ha. I laugh politely. "Okay, I'll try," I say.

What I should do is storm off and quit. But can't. My ego holds me back. Every now and then a half decent cartoon sneaks by and I'm ecstatic. One morning not long after the "ap-PEEL-ing" incident, I drive up to Cumberland Farms to get the newspaper as always. Before buying it I sneak my usual nervous look at the editorial page. And there it is! In the prime spot. Right next to the editorials, and reproduced quite well, reduced by only 40%.

I wait until I'm in the parking lot to do my victory jig. I dance in little circles with the paper above my head. Then I stop and pretend to be the average newspaper reader. I skim the front page, glancing at the funnies and sports, finally taking a look at the editorial page. Hmmmmm, what's this? What a fine cartoon. Yes, a cartoon by Gessner. Quite good. I'll have to remember that name.

I drive away almost forgetting to get copies, then drive back to pick up six more.

~

Even as I stamp and mail the letter, I'm sure of its fate. I know the Cape Cod *Times* well enough to know they'll never print it.

Still, it feels good to send. Like so many people, my outrage muscles have atrophied. Sure I mutter as I watch the news, but what is personal outrage if not an oxymoron? Without public action, outrage is just impotent rage.

I rationalize that cartoons and essays are my way of flexing, but that's a cop-out. I'm no pillar of righteousness. My cartoons may have attacked the Cape's attackers, but what motivated me? The same sort of ambition that drives my so-called enemies.

As for essays, who reads them? I mean that seriously. "I don't see any sense of preaching," the Western poet and essayist Reg Saner told me. "If they're reading this kind of work then they already believe this stuff anyway." I don't have the same ability to suppress my lecturing, but he's right. Why preach to the converted?

When we turn to both nature essays and political cartoons, we expect to find outrage. And if outrage becomes merely a genre, we're in trouble. Where can life and blood be found if not in outrage?

In his introduction to his own work in The Gang of Eight, *Don Wright, the editorial cartoonist for the Miami* News, *talks about the sorry state of editorial cartooning today. Most cartoonists, he says, are content to produce,*

reams of uninspired, no, worse, "funny" little figures acting out some half-baked, often obscure caption. Gone is the pamphleteering spirit of our revolutionary ancestors, to whom debate and political controversy were noble persuasions. . . . Are we really artists or simply an occasional, but passionless, filler in a nervous newspaper?

I know what I am. I'm becoming the master of passionless filler, working for a paper that's nervous to the point of epilepsy. I'm guilty as charged. I talk a good game, but what's the reality? I stand terrified—knees wobbling—before my slight, insectlike editor, trembling as if facing a dragon. Worse, I do his bidding. Yesterday, I brought him a picture of two giant, anthropomorphized gypsy moths in a Volkswagen. The moths were trying to sneak onto a ferry and migrate to Martha's Vineyard (chortle, chortle). When I showed it to him, a smile broke across his face. "Now you're thinking!" he said. His actual words.

And so the old question: What is to be done?

What, for instance, can I do about the idiots overdeveloping Cape Cod? Edward Abbey would have told me that eco-defense is the answer. The earth is our home, and if our home is being destroyed we have the right to defend ourselves:

> If a stranger batters your door down with an axe, threatens your family and yourself with deadly weapons, and proceeds to loot your home of whatever he wants, he is committing what is universally recognized—by law and common morality—as a crime. In such a situation the householder has both the right and the obligation to defend himself, his family, and his property by whatever means necessary.

Abbey urged us to do what it takes to stop the building: cut down billboards, pour sand in tractors' gas tanks, spike trees with sixty-penny nails, and pull up developer's stakes.

I make it a habit to pull up stakes, but the rest really isn't my style. Maybe Abbey's environmentalism doesn't transplant well, and is best kept in the West. Here, living closer together, my enemies are also my friends. I can't quite see pouring sand into Chris Cooney's tractors, and though he sometimes cheats in tennis I'd never set fire to Donald Patterson's monstrosity of a house.

The last straw.

"I think you've gone overboard on these environmental issues," the editor tells me, "there's no sense beating a dead horse."

I can barely believe the words as they come out of his mouth. Isn't horse beating the whole point of political cartooning? Every good cartoonist is a horse beater. The best always sniff the air for rotting flesh, always ready to pounce when a horse goes down, ready to beat and beat and beat.

A political cartoonist, is, after all, a particular sort of extremist. A fanatic with a smile. Every day he must take an issue and be a bore with it, must sit down at his toy piano and hit the same

note over and over, over and over, until it's annoying, then even-
tually more annoying, and then, finally, funny. Attacking with
the same caricatures, the same mind-set, the same themes, day
after day after day. Attacking while knowing that, meanwhile,
all over the country, there are hundreds of other cartoonists hit-
ting their readers over the head with the same points, the same
styles, and sometimes, the same actual cartoons. Attacking as
an individual piece of a larger unoriginal art form—an art form
featuring inbreeding that would make a mountain clan blush—
as a part of a great communal and anonymous horse beating. A
collective ceremony. Hundreds of ignored and silly preachers,
beating away, preaching and pounding. All together. Building up
to a frenzy. Beating, beating, beating.

"Horse beating required" should be the first line in a political
cartoonist's job description. If these editors would let me, just
once, I'd show them what that phrase means. I'd roll up my
sleeves and slam with my fists. I'd mash the bloody equine in-
testines, punching again and again. I'd kiss the bruises on my
knuckles. I'd relish the whole business, the gruesome entrails,
the slaughterhouse stink. . . . Yes, I'd love my work. I'd pound
and pound and pound.

Maybe we're too sophisticated for outrage. After all, even the
stylistic choice is extreme—the language we're required to use is
hyperbolic, rhetorical. Certainly polemics are out of vogue,
gauche. When we're righteous we risk becoming ridiculous.

Maybe we're too able to see all sides. Outrage requires simpli-
fying our views.

When I quit, it isn't melodramatic. Nothing confrontational,
none of the angry scenes I'd imagined. I simply tell them, "I'm
moving on," and they wish me good luck.

But once home I indulge a theatrical impulse. I open the plas-
tic sheathing of my portfolio case and separate the "appealing"
cartoons from my stronger work. I stack them neatly, tapping
them against the top of the wood stove like a deck of cards.

I drop a cartoon from the stack into the mouth of the wood stove. Then, one by one, I drop the rest into the fire. White and black ink explode into orange and blue. I feed the fire until it's raging, leaping and nipping at my hands. I watch my work burn and feel strangely happy.

What is to be done?

Get angry. And let anger beget action.

But what sort of action? I'm no Robin Hood, no monkey wrencher. Maybe, despite the cancer rates and environmental threats, the answer is to connect myself even more to this place, to East Dennis. To do whatever I can: write letters, draw cartoons, go to town meetings. To root myself here. To commit, even if it is to sandy, polluted soil.

But why *here*?

It's simple really. Because this is where I feel most at home, and, while my methods aren't as dramatic as his, I agree with Ed Abbey. We must defend our home.

NEIGHBORS

✦

I t's shaggier, bushier than I expected. Clearly not a dog. I only catch a quick glimpse before it ducks off into the trees on our property. Its thick gray tail disappears behind the pear tree. The Western trickster has followed me east. How strange to see a coyote on Cape Cod. My occasional sightings in the foot-hills of the Rockies were exciting, but this is something different altogether. Wildness among the divided lots, sand, and abandoned summer homes.

Last night I ate dinner at Heidi Schadt's. There isn't any place I feel more at home. Heidi is the salt of the earth. Or of the sea, I should say, considering the years she's spent here. Thoreau wrote that Cape people have a "broad and invulnerable good humour." I think of Heidi's wonderful ruddy face that can, at any second, blurt out a loud flat *"ha-ha"* laugh sure to embarrass her daugh-ters. It's a laugh capable of stopping conversation in restaurants, a laugh of pure outgoing pleasure that puts me immediately at ease and lets me know I'm on the Cape.

Last night she talked about growing up on Cape Cod and then getting married and moving to a farm in Pennsylvania. When she returned to the Cape, without her husband but with four kids, Heidi tried to bring pieces of the farm back with her. She kept chickens and pigs and goats in her backyard, until the neighbors and zoning board found out about it. One winter, working as a carpenter and depressed from being alone in my icebox of a house, I asked if I could stay in her spare bedroom. Her house wasn't much warmer than mine, but it was infinitely cozier.

Heidi gave me some advice that winter: "Always keep living things around you." She kept her own counsel. Besides her two daughters, who lived at home, there were cats and dogs and still a few chickens. Sitting in front of the wood stove with Heidi and Becky and Elizabeth, I'd settle back on pillows and stare happily at the TV. In exchange for my paying the absurdly low rent and chopping and bringing in wood, Heidi cooked me huge fatty dinners from another era; plates heaped with potatoes dripping with butter, Flintstone-sized pork chops, and tubs of vanilla ice cream for dessert. Then when I went through the pantomime of trying to help clean the dishes she would practically push me back down in the chair. "No, no, no, no," she'd bluster. "You're our guest. The girls will wash the dishes."

While living things filled the upstairs of Heidi's house, dead things filled the basement.

The basement was the province of Heidi's only son, Danny, and it was there he kept his skins. From nails in the cellar walls hung tyrannosaurus-jawed metal traps and the furs of raccoons, woodchucks, and beavers. As a teenager Danny roamed the marsh and creeks, setting traps and collecting dead animals in his pouch. I called him Trapper Dan.

I get up at five, pull on my clothes, and head for the marsh. My quick glimpse will now turn into a methodical search. I want to see the coyote again.

At the harbor the birds are riotous. An eggcup moon leads me across the marsh, through high tick grasses and spongy glasswort. The glasswort grows in patches of not quite olive green. I read somewhere that the plant was sought out by settlers to add to their salads. I chew on a piece. It's a little salty thanks to the ocean, but it does have a crisp celery taste.

A salt river trickles through the heart of the marsh, dribbling down a waterfall of muck. Here the marsh is ringed by eastern red cedar, briars, and a dilapidated stone wall. An old catboat called the *Clovelly* decays on the hill behind the wall. The grass grows wildly around the boat, yellowed hair matted and strewn down muddy banks. Near where I sit the taller brown grass is mottled sideways, as if an elephant had been napping there. No sign of the coyote.

Trapper Dan is now almost thirty years old. He manages the Sesuit Marina across the street from my house. He's a big man

with a chest as square and solid as a wood stove. Most of the time he's quiet. He's never talked much, even as a kid, but underneath his quiet is a deep reservoir of humor and intelligence. Sometimes I can hear his laugh all the way up at my house—it's a burlier, baritone version of Heidi's.

Danny moved from the farm to the Cape when he was eleven, a vulnerable age to leave your father behind. At first he was uneasy here, and painfully shy. Trapping was one of the ways he began to feel comfortable.

Another dawn walk in search of the coyote. Today the tide is low enough to cross the entire marsh. I do, and, after my fruitless search, have breakfast on the other side, at Marshside.

Bitter coffee, sausage, eggs, toast. I sit next to a man with the neck and nose of a mud turtle. He orders: "a chocolate donut and a side order of home fries."

He turns to me and smiles.

"I like potatoes for breakfast," he says.

~

A few years after Danny first moved here, Sammy Mack became an important figure in his life. Sammy was the town's harbormaster, but had had a thousand other jobs. He ran a gas station, had an underwater salvage business, captained a tuna boat, took care of most of the lawns on the neck, plowed snow, sold wood, fixed boats and cars, and would do almost anything else. He was a short man with manic energy and a puckish, crazy smile, and as a kid I was impressed by his bulging Popeye forearms. I'm sure Danny Schadt was, too. Not long after Sammy came around Danny started lifting weights.

Why was Sammy around? He was friends with Heidi. I sometimes wonder how much of that relationship was calculated on her part—the need to have a man nearby for her growing son. Whatever the reason behind his presence, Sammy became the ringmaster of our little world. Heidi's garage—our meeting place—spilled over with scuba gear and tools and motorcycle parts and various gizmos (even a one-man submarine) from Sammy's projects and jobs. Sammy would round up the Schadt and Gessner children and lead us on adventures. One day we might go diving for treasure in Scargo Lake—not imaginary treasure chests but real treasure, like lost watches. Another day we might feed Heidi's pigs with garbage from Marshside, or cut wood illegally behind Scargo Tower. Whatever he was doing, Sammy let out little war whoops and yips, or shifted abruptly into different voices, like Robin Williams.

I was a nervous kid, never completely comfortable working with Sammy, and he and the Schadts cast me in the role of the book-smart city boy with no common sense. They laughed when I didn't know how to pump gas at a self-serve or start a chainsaw, and I laughed, too. I developed a self-depreciating routine.

But where I flailed, Danny flourished. He was practical. He excelled at working with motors and tools and gizmos—all things grubby and manly. And Sammy's craziness taught him to laugh again.

I drive down to the natural-history museum. I find an article by Peter Trull about how the coyote returned to Cape Cod. By the late 1970s the coyotes were well established in western Massachusetts. The coyote "was—and is—a path follower" and the paths they followed were the obvious ones. It's quite likely that the coyotes got to the Cape just like every other tourist—by taking Route 3 or 495. How did they cross the bridge? Apparently they used the same technique I used when I commuted to Boston from the Cape on summer weekends. I'd nap in the day to avoid the heavy traffic, then drive back in the middle of the night. The coyotes waited to avoid traffic, too. Then, in the dead of the night, they simply jogged over the bridge.

Before heading home, I hike down one of the museum's trails. Not expecting to see a coyote, hardly expecting to see anything, I emerge from a tunnel of trees into marshland and am shocked out of self. A blaze of white soars right above me, crossing and climbing higher. An osprey lets out its hawk cry. I stand perfectly still and watch as it circles downward before landing in its nest. The nest stands on a manmade platform in the middle of the marsh, built of actual branches, not sticks. It, like the bird itself, seems startlingly large.

Once almost wiped out by DDT and other pesticides, ospreys have escaped the endangered-species list and, like the coyote, returned to the Cape.

When I was in my late teens I spent a summer working on Sammy's tuna boat, which looked as if it had been nailed and lashed together from random scraps.

Each day Sammy stocked the boat's cooler with beers, though he didn't drink himself. "Look what I've got for my first mate," he announced every morning. He would spring down elf-like to the deck and open the cooler as if it were a treasure chest, showing me the glimmering cans of Busch or Bud on ice.

I stayed drunk most of the summer and we never caught a single tuna. Still I have pleasant memories of driving the boat while Sammy stayed up in the pulpit on the bowsprit, harpoon in hand. At the end of each unsuccessful day, we headed back toward the harbor, Sammy leaning out over the water and steering with his foot, while I stayed up in the crow's nest watching the sun sizzle into the water. When it was dark I'd come down and he'd cook

Dinty Moore beef stew on the Bunsen burner. Occasionally I still buy Dinty Moore, but it always tastes congealed and processed, never the hearty, warming stew of that summer.

Unseasonably warm. My friend Hones comes down from Watertown for a weekend of drinking and eating. He also brings along a dozen books on coyote myths from the Boston Public Library.

Hung over on Sunday, I drag Hones out of bed at dawn for my daily search. After our unsuccessful watch ends, we head down to the little beach. A military array greets us. As we walk out on the jetty, the birds take off in perfect ranks. They swoop out toward the bay, bank and roll as if on command—become silver flecks in the sun—then bank and return, landing thirty yards behind us. We reverse direction and walk toward them; they take off and repeat the show. This time one bird slips up on the turn, but then performs a beautiful roll of its own, angles in and cuts off the pack, returning to its appointed place. I've seen the navy's Blue Angels fly, and I was impressed, but these pipers are even more precise.

On the way back home we dig into the muck and fill a sack with mussels. When we have enough, we wash them off at the town pier; they shine metallic blue. Hones follows a recipe from an old cookbook. We dip the mussels in broth and butter, and drink a dozen weiss beers. For dessert we eat oranges.

After Hones passes out on the couch, I lose myself in the books of myths. Coyote is everywhere. Mocking, deceiving, conniving, helping, and falling flat on his vaudevillian face. Among the Interior Salish of the Northwest he is called Sin-Ka-liṗ, the imitator. The Brule Sioux tell of him cheating a cheater of his clothes and horse, and in a White Mountain Apache story Coyote fights a lump of pitch put out by a farmer whose wheat he has been stealing. Spokane, Nez Perce, Kalapuya, Wintu, Pima. So many tribes with so many stories about this half-hero, half-buffoon. In a Crow myth coyote makes the world, and the California Maidu tell a story of how he creates death, only to have his son step on a snake and be the first to die.

Coyote is always asking for trouble. In one story he outsmarts Bear, in the next, a Tewa Pueblo myth, he is bested by Badger. He challenges Badger to a hunting match, wagering a night with the other's wife. Of course, in tortoise-and-hair fashion, Coyote speeds about all day—when not napping and daydreaming of intercourse with Badger-woman—only to return with one pelt, while badger ploddingly collects many. That night Coyote must stand outside his home while Coyote-woman screams from painful intercourse with Badger and his horrible drill-shaped penis.

Sammy cares fiercely about making money, but there's always a sense that making mischief is even more important.

Maybe Sammy is our local trickster.

Why, outside of his general sense of mischief, does he remind me of Coyote? Because there's something slinking, modern, crass about him. For all Sammy's fun, he's out for a buck. And for all his rebelliousness, he kowtows to the powerful summer people. That's his way of surviving.

Coyote represents what is "creative, unpredictable, contradictory" in us, says poet Gary Snyder. Coyote has a little P. T. Barnum in him. In a White Mountain Apache myth he ties a bag of money to a tree and sells it to a gullible group of men as a money tree. He sticks a coin up a donkey's ass, lets it shit out the coin, then sells it to the big man in town as a gold-shitting ass. Coyote is always in trouble, but always sneaking out of it. He gets drunk, gets thrown in jail, cheats his way to freedom.

There is a wildness to Coyote, but it's a modern wildness. The crass wildness of the gambler, the drunkard, the antihero, the swindler. A civilized, unwild wild.

The real wild man on the neck isn't Sammy, but my next-door neighbor, Seth. Legends circle around Seth, a big man who was once a heavyweight boxer. There are stories of how he knocked a policeman to the ground, how he jumped over a moving car that was trying to run him down, and how his dogs drowned a police shepherd in the cranberry bog. It's said that once he threw the old marina manager—the one before Danny—off the docks and into the water.

These stories aside, our family always got along well with him. I went up to his house every now and then when I was a kid. Seth taught me how to ride a horse and throw a lacrosse ball. He also taught me to box. I hit the heavy bag in his barn, staring up at tattered sepia posters of faded boxers. The bag barely moved when I hit it, but swung and shook when Seth punched. By that time Seth was even more of a heavyweight than in his fighting days, particularly around the middle, and he was every inch a red head. He had a wild beard, and red hair curled out of his nostrils, down his cheeks and chin, climbing over his throat, working its way around his neck and gathering in a thick doormat on his upper back. The only place it was missing was on the very top of his head.

When I was a little older I helped Seth hammer down the roof of his barn. He relieved the tedium of the work by throwing things around and yelling whatever came into his head. His voice was loud, loud enough to be heard over the din of power tools. The muscles, beneath the red, matted hair, were not the kind you get from a Nautilus machine. The skin of his right forearm bulged like a thin paper bag overstuffed with twelve-penny nails.

When I returned to the Cape in my twenties, I saw Seth as a kind of exaggerated reflection of myself. His father had been a famous surgeon and had bought the house for him. In my head, Seth was the rebellious son, living in his fortress up on the hill, surrounded by trees, a chain across his driveway to keep all others away.

Seth was reclusive, but sometimes I bumped into him around town. During a blizzard he lifted my AMC Spirit out of a snowbank. Once I saw him outside of the post office as we splashed through a puddle, moving in opposite directions.

"Nice day," he yelled at me, "—for ducks!"

It wasn't the comment itself that was odd, but what he did next. He let go with a wild, bleating goat laugh, his wide-open mouth revealing a set of yellow chipped teeth that clung to his gums like barnacles. There was a tension in him that seemed to originate in his upper back, twist and travel around his neck, and find its full focus in his eyes.

When I saw him later that day in Cumberland Farms, he feigned amazement.

"You're like stink," he yelled over the Hostess counter. "You're everywhere!"

The other day I asked Danny if he'd ever seen a coyote.

"Hundreds," he said.

I nodded seriously, accepting his answer, then looked at him again. A small smile barely curled at the ends of his lips.

"Really?" I asked.

"No, not really." He laughed the Schadt laugh, easily audible across the harbor. I laughed, too, and walked away. But then Danny called me back.

"I saw some last spring, David," he said quietly, pointing toward the marsh. "A litter of pups in the heather near that old catboat."

~

Seth and Sammy despised each other. Why? Maybe because, despite their strains of wildness, they played by a different set of rules. Or rather Seth didn't play by rules at all, while Sammy knew the rules well.

They had several conflicts down at the docks, culminating in a final clash straight out of Native American mythology: Coyote versus Bear. The way I heard it, Seth was walking along the town dock when he saw Sammy cleaning his tuna boat. He went up to the boat and began bellowing at Sammy over some prior grievance.

"If I ever catch you off that boat," he yelled. "I'll kill you."

Sammy stepped right off the boat and said, "Here I am." Seth's punch almost knocked him off the dock.

But while Bear used raw force, Coyote used cunning and his knowledge of the white man's ways. Sammy took Seth to court. And in the end Coyote got his way. Seth's sentence was a harsh one. He was banished from the town of East Dennis.

Dinner at Heidi's again. Tonight a big steak.

Looking for a beer I open the fridge door. And stare. Heidi is the queen of excess. She just went shopping and her fridge bulges and throbs, burgeoning and grotesque. Inside it's a carnivore's delight, with enough meat to rival a deli. Roast beef, turkey, ham, good beef bologna stacked high. A dish piled with leftover pork chops, hardened over with delicious grease. Sausages, marmalade, grape jelly. Strange surprises half-covered in foil. Blueberry muffins? Corn bread? Eight eggs and a package of meat—by feel, ground beef—wrapped in white butcher's paper. In the nether regions, a member of the eggplant/lasagna family, now hard and withered. A dinner plate smeared with butter. A pitcher of aged iced tea; melons, grapefruit, lettuce, the remains of last night's salad, tasting even better after hours spent soaking in oil and vinegar. And mayonnaise . . . enough mayonnaise to clog the arteries of a battalion.

When I lived here I worried that food would go bad because the fridge door couldn't possibly be closed. Now I manage to close it and walk back to the living room with my beer.

Danny is sitting in the stiff-backed rocking chair. He smiles. "David, you trap any Kī-yots yet?" he asks.

The image of me as a coyote trapper ripples laughter through the Schadt family. Elizabeth and Becky laugh at fairly normal decibels, while Heidi and Danny shake the walls of the house.

I laugh, too. The Schadts always help me get outside of myself. When I lived here, I'd get a certain look on my face and Heidi knew I was overanalyzing. She'd then put her hand on my shoulder. "Stop it, David," she'd say. "You worry too much." Somehow, coming from her, the advice didn't seem trite. Occasionally, I actually stopped worrying.

Soon we're devouring dinner. Danny is at the head of the table near the living room, Heidi at the head near the kitchen. As she dishes out enormous portions, I remember a fictional character I once based loosely on Heidi. I called her Eliza Bulwark. Eliza's features were hard and wooden. She had a long nose like a keel, and sharp lines formed points as they turned the corners of the face. Her rigid profile jutted forward, like a figurehead riding the prow of a clipper ship. Eliza would have been right at home cutting through the salty breakers, never flinching.

Eliza was a serviceable character, but she wasn't Heidi. Heidi's face is smooth and joyful; her features are softer, as if worn down gently by the ocean like the sea glass you find at the shore. Eliza was tough to the point of meanness. Heidi's is a different kind of toughness—a soft, mothering toughness. She is a survivor because she's had to be, but never at the expense of humor and warmth, never at the expense of her love of living things.

Up at dawn again despite my slight hangover. Why? I'm not sure.

Today I head out through the marina to the little beach. Ducks wake with a ruffling explosion as I approach. In the sky, below a vertebrae of blue, a line glowing orange-red winds like a trail over rough ground. The numbered docks, coated with last season's chipped gray paint, are out of the water, piled up in the harbor parking lot.

At the beach, the wind and cold are almost overpowering. Stars shine behind the waving, interweaving eelgrass. In the hazy dawn light the breakers roll in a gripping, cleansing white.

Having no luck at the beach, I double back to the marsh. We've been told the marsh is a sickly place, the home of disease and ticks, and, after the bracing cold of the beach, it does seem sick. With each footstep I feel as if I'm breaking eggshells and then walking through the ooze of yolk. When I reach the decaying cat-boat, I triple-check for ticks.

Leaning on the gunwale of the boat, I listen to the whispering of Spartina grass. Another voice, this one from inside, tells me that I'll keep coming out here each morning, hoping for a closer look at the coyote. Why? Because I want to see the mythic trick-ster's face. I imagine it might have my father's beaming, mis-chievous eyes.

HERRING, VAN GOGH, AND ME

Work is the only remedy; if that does
not help, one breaks down.
—Vincent van Gogh

🖋

In late April the herring return to Cape Cod. Today I take the seven-minute drive to Brewster, hoping to see this spectacle once again. The herring, or alewives as they're sometimes called, are anadromous—Greek for "up running." Every year they return from the sea to their freshwater birthplace.

As I climb out of the car, I'm hit by the smell, the stream stinking of fish. It's a weekend and tourists in gaudy Bermuda shorts and green alligator shirts pack the water's edge. Their offspring emit harsh yells, harass the fish, chase each other, slam into strangers. The water is also alive with movement, foaming and frothing, the herring thrilling it with their upward twisting.

I follow the path running parallel to the stream, past the old mill with its churning waterwheel. This stretch contains the last hurdles before the fish return to the pond where they were born, and where they'll soon spawn. Silver flecks and flashes light the dark water, hundreds of fish hurling themselves up seemingly insurmountable rapids. From above come hectoring calls even more grating than those of the children. Dozens of gulls hover, swooping down at their leisure to snack on the struggling herring. It seems particularly unfair when a bird spears a fish that's only a few feet from its final goal. But the herring hardly notice the grisly deaths of their companions, so intent are they on their mission. Nothing matters but throwing themselves up the next hurdle, a feat comparable, in human terms, to swimming up a waterfall.

In human terms. I watch a burly, bearded man in an Adidas warm-up suit lean out over the water. There is a sign posted nearby warning that it's illegal to impede the herring's progress, but by the look in his eyes it doesn't seem impossible that the

man can't read. He reaches out with one bear-paw hand and stabs it into the water like a fishing grizzly. He stabs unsuccessfully several times, a cartoon look of consternation coming over his face. When he finally spears a fish he holds it up and waves it to the crowd. "I got one," he yells. "I got one!"

I move down the stream, bristling with happy moral superiority. After a little while, I forget the man and find myself focusing on one particular herring. I root it on. I ward off gulls as it circles in a small pool with a dozen other fish, resting before attacking the rapids again. It leaps up into the white rush of water, only to be thrown back down to the pool. I'm thinking that first leap, when the fish is rested and its energy is at its highest, will be its best shot. But my herring thinks differently. It throws itself right back, again and again, until somehow, on its eighth attempt, it breaks though the powerful rush of water. I cheer, but my fish has no time to gloat. It now faces a ledge of flowing water even higher and more powerful than the last, and, after a three-second rest, throws itself into the froth.

It's out of vogue to make symbols of nature, to ascribe human emotions to animals, but watching this relentless upward charge, trying to fathom this fathomless motivation, I can't help but give the fish a human face. As I stare, my herring begins to transform. Its dark forehead scrunches with determination. Its face distorts with intensity. Its scales writhe and shine silver. Then, finally, strangely, it grows a goatee and a small swath of red hair.

I discovered my herring's face in college.

It was a face that I'd later see everywhere, a pop-culture cliché staring out from posters, calendars, and movies. But when I first saw it, during my junior year, I was a relative innocent. At the time, wandering into the Fogg Art Museum, my interests were restricted to literature, Ultimate Frisbee, and drinking. Moving quickly through the bottom floor, I gave most of the paintings perfunctory looks. I became mildly interested in the overblown landscapes of the early American Romantics, admiring their scope but thinking they lacked action (and waves). I was ready to leave when I passed the entrance to a room on the second floor. Even before I entered the room, I saw the painting. It hung on the opposite wall, twenty feet away.

At first it seemed less a painting than an actual man, a neighbor seen through a window frame. He stood there in his kitchen, by the dishes, looking out at my world as clearly as I looked into his. I walked up to the window and stared through it. The atmosphere inside was throbbing. The face bristled, looking tight and constrained, painfully intense. I wanted to take a wet cloth to the face. Browns and greens swirled from the borders of the painting in toward the vortex of the face, while at the same time a vibrating force emanated from the man's skin. Swirling in, emanating out. And the color. The dominant color was malachite green. Unearthly and strange and perfect.

The painting was van Gogh's self-portrait of September 1888, dedicated to his by-then tormenter, Paul Gauguin. What made the world inside it so real, I decided, was the thickness of the paint. It was piled there, lumped and uneven, as if still, almost a hundred years later, it hadn't quite dried. It looked like it had been left unfinished, waiting for the painter to return to it later in the day. Unlike the other paintings I'd seen, I could easily imagine an actual man creating this, could genuinely picture how he might have done it.

I stood in front of my painting for half an hour, boxing out other patrons. Then, right before I left, I did something unconscionable. There was a knot of wood in the middle of the canvas that had been incorporated into the work, becoming the top button of van Gogh's shirt. The knot jutted far off the surface of the canvas, farther out than even the thickest globs of paint. I glanced behind me. The guard strolled out toward an adjacent room filled with modern statues. I was breathless, but I knew that I'd do it. Quickly, lightly, I touched the knot with my right forefinger. Even with that one light brush of a fingertip, it felt surprisingly solid, like bone or a clump of hair. I stepped back from the painting, pretending I'd only been looking. No one was the wiser for my transgression.

I began to dream of creating something just as intense, just as alive. I decided to write a novel. It would be an honest book in which I'd paint the world around me in vivid and crude colors.

I worked and worked, but couldn't get it right. I wanted my words to be simple and honest, but everything I wrote seemed stilted and disingenuous. I never found an angle into my material or, more to the point, found too many angles, writing the novel in every conceivable fashion from every conceivable point of view. I had many titles, but might have aptly called the book *Quagmire*. It was large, awkward, unwieldy, and, it turned out, entirely unpublishable. While I wrote, I worked as a bookstore clerk and carpenter's apprentice, making less than ten-thousand dollars a year. I felt a growing sense of panic and failure.

It was during those difficult years that van Gogh became one of my heroes—all the rest of whom, excluding Larry Bird, were literary. I bought a large secondhand book of his prints, a paperback copy of his letters, and a biography by Julius Meir-Graefe. I loved immersing myself in the painter's world. It was a nervous, edgy world, a world you could feel gyrating around you. I particularly enjoyed the jitteriness. It was like drinking too much coffee, a shaking but deliciously out-of-control pleasure bordering on sickness.

I kept the Meir-Graefe biography by my bedside and read from it before sleep:

His modesty was well founded. His talent seemed extraordinarily small. Scores of mediocrities started with greater gifts. He drew like a boy of twelve, not a line was straight, and in his drawings one can almost see his awkward fingers tracing the lines across the paper.

The words filled me with hope. Van Gogh hadn't even begun to paint until he was twenty-seven! If *he* could achieve something great with so little promise, perhaps I could, too. If I worked hard enough. That was the chief lesson I took from him. Art as work. I sat as if chained to the leg of my desk, with its porthole window looking out at freedom and Cape Cod Bay, and tried to will sentences into existence. If I needed encouragement, I turned to the letters. They reinforced my sense of the need for hard, disciplined labor. Again and again van Gogh's words stressed the importance of willpower, of naked persistence:

For great things are not done by impulse, but by a series of small things brought together. And great things are not accidental, but must certainly be *willed*. What is drawing? How does one learn it? It is working through an invisible iron wall that seems to stand between what one feels and what one can do.

It was hard to read van Gogh's letters and not be infected with a similar vocabulary, with his sense of art not only as work, but also as war, a life or death struggle. The tone is aggressive, a vocabulary of attack:

The imagination is made keener and more correct by continually studying nature and *wrestling* with it. . . . I have no doubt, no hesitation in attacking things. . . . to swallow that despair and melancholy, to hear oneself as one is, not in order to sit down and rest but to struggle on, notwithstanding thousands of shortcomings and faults, and the doubtfulness of conquering them. . . . To be in the open air and to work with animation are things that renew and keep our strength. . . . one feels a power surging within; one has work to do and it must be done. . . . Taking a rest is out of the question, so I keep at my work as best I can.

I started writing notes to myself about attacking my novel, about *charging, flinging, throwing* myself into it. I sat in the attic of the Cape house glaring out at the blue-black winter sea, working to the coffee machine's puttering as I muttered vows to myself: "I will *work* and *work* and *work*."

I look away for a minute and my herring is gone, lost in a numberless, faceless gang. No more red hair. No more goatee. No more scrunched forehead. If it's dubious to make symbols of nature, then it's doubly so to make these fish into a metaphor of individual struggle. They move past me in a squiggling black mass. In *The Atlantic Shore*, John Hay and Peter Farb wrote of the alewives: "They climb the frothing torrents, vibrantly, persistently. The reproductive power of the sea is in them, a relentless drive that carries with it a risk, a precarious balance."

What motivated van Gogh? A relentless drive, certainly. But instinctive? These last hundred-plus years have been poor ones for the concept of free will, but if ever we feel a will at work it's in van Gogh's letters. His fight with mental illness, his profound loneliness, his anguish and urge for beauty all come through desperately. Isn't this acute consciousness—driving through "an invisible iron wall"—quite the opposite of what we call instinct? Or is the element of self-consciousness, of language, the only difference?

The clichéd answer to the question, "Why do you write?" is "Because I have to." I've said it, too. Is this a trite response or is there really something to it? Do we really have to? What does it mean to be driven? The herring are compelled to return to their parent stream to spawn by forces deep within them. I tell myself that I'm not driven in this way, but, on second thought, there's an obvious comparison. I keep returning to Cape Cod, both as physical place and subject matter. For years I've told myself that I could write about other things, could consciously attach myself to another place. But all the while I find myself coming back to the Cape. I return to my father's house, to my own parent stream.

John Hay has a word for what drives the herring: memory. An "inherited, racial" memory learned from others of its species, a memory hundreds, thousands, of years old. I can't say if some drive to use language as art is encoded in our species, but I do know that conscious memory is part of what drives me to write. Walter Jackson Bate speaks of the uses of tradition, of man's freedom "to follow openly and directly what he most values: what he has been taught to value, what he secretly or openly wishes he had done or could do."

For years, while working in this attic study, I have taped pictures and quotes of my heroes on the wall in front of me. Van Gogh, Samuel Johnson, Thoreau, Keats, Montaigne. Tradition points the way. Their words and images act as pulls and prods. They drive me onward.

I watch sheer glistening movement as the herring climb walls of water. The copper-colored stream bubbles with constant twisting, the blue sheen of a hundred dorsal fins slicing the surface. The fins flicker, sometimes carving above the water like miniature shark attacks, broiling the creek with foam. The fish change colors, one second a silver-belted blue, the next a purple crosshatching, then the white flashing of bellies.

Hundreds of shadows fill the stream. The herring need their vast numbers to insure success. "Fish are the embodiment of abundance," wrote Hay and Farb, "it is a necessity for their survival."

I live inside a spinning narcissistic world, constantly creating my own day-to-day drama. I convince myself of my work's importance, in part to have the energy necessary to tackle it—so I can throw myself at it again and again. But though I often feel alone, I am anything but. I'm one of a species, almost a cliché: the struggling young writer off in his garret, wrought up over his own work and existence.

Currently I'm on leave from a master's program in creative writing. While programs such as this hardly existed twenty years ago, they've now sprouted up all over the country. So many of us crowding the graduate schools, all with the same ambitions and delusions, each individual believing he or she is somehow blessed, or at the very least "gifted." We, too, are the embodiment of abundance. A desperate squiggling mass. I laugh, thinking that maybe there *is* a need for so many of us to believe we can make it, so that a few actually can.

In recent years van Gogh is the fish who made it. Calendar boy, media superstar—as cursed by popularity in our time as by unpopularity in his own. Everyone knows his life. The buzzwords are in place: Madness. Arles. The Ear. No sales. A failure during the nineteenth century, in the twentieth he has it all: movies and millions.

What should we make of this? Of van Gogh's almost complete lack of success while he was alive? The fact is often mentioned, seldom dwelt on. Who wants to dwell on it? Unless we believe in a heaven, where van Gogh now sits, fat, happy, and popular, we can see no point, no justice.

How many worked just as hard as van Gogh whom we have never heard of? This question edges me fearfully closer to my own ultimate doubts. I see friends moving ahead in their careers, and fear I'm being left behind. I now have a cardboard Budweiser case full of rejections. I worry: what if after all this work, nothing comes of it? What if I don't have the talent? Couldn't the idea of persistence prove dangerous—even disastrous—for the wrong person? If we really don't have the talent, or the luck, does all the persistence in the world make a difference? What if van Gogh worked just as fervently but had not been van Gogh?

I turn to the letters for help. There I find constant unending struggle as its own reward:

> Just then I feel what work is to me, how it gives tone to life, apart from approval or disapproval; and on days that would otherwise make one melancholy, one is glad to have an aim.

I nod as I read. It's healthy to work hard at things others consider ridiculous, even if it comes to nothing. Work for its own sake. I *like* banging my head against a wall.

It begins to rain, driving away the bright-colored tourists and making the water's surface even choppier. I stay and watch the herring swim against the current, a violent, jerky climb. I take notes trying to describe them, but they're hard to pin a color on. Greens, grays, browns, flashes of silver, yellow, even red. Van Gogh could have painted the herring. I remember again the painting of his I saw in Zurich, a trout with its back lit with silver dashing strokes—iridescent, many colored. I would have liked to touch that painting, if only for a second. The brush strokes were so rough, it seemed his intention had not been merely to paint, but to gouge.

Downstream, instead of rocks, the fish jump through manmade ladders—cement walls with "entrances" cut into their middles. These aren't friendly entrances: the stream gushes loudly down though them. While a few fish throw themselves up into the rush, the others wait, circling and gathering energy, moving with the same fluidity as the water.

Water is the central fact of the herring's existence. It surrounds them, courses over them, fights against them. It's the herring's medium. The natural analogy would be to say that people live in air, but today I think of something else. Words. We are born into them and live in them. We writhe through them sinuously, moving upward as they rush over and purl around us. We can't get rid of them even when we want to. They fill us, bubbling up like springs in our minds. While most of us can't paint or play an instrument, we all have words. Perhaps van Gogh was most comfortable with paint, with color, but even he spilled out pages and pages of letters to his brother Theo almost every night. For most of us words are the medium. Our everyday art and common heritage.

By the side of the stream, more words. A sign:

Warning. No person shall remove, take, or obstruct passage of the herring during Friday, Saturday, Sunday. Police will prosecute.

—Laws, Chapter 131.

I laugh. Our men in blue protecting the herring. Nice, too, that Sunday is a day of rest from at least their human predators, though neither the gulls nor eels likely take the day off.

There is another sign a few feet upstream:

In memory of Ernie Gage, a member of the alewife committee and Stoney Brook committee, in recognition of his longstanding and tireless effort in preserving the herring run and millsite.

Effort, longstanding and tireless. Were these words chosen consciously?

My clothes are soaked by the time I head back to the car. I drive up Stoney Brook Road, past the church and Red Top cemetery with its waferlike gravestones, take a left on 6-A, a route as familiar and comfortable as my own driveway. When I get home, I hurry upstairs to my study to scribble down a few notes in my journal. "Don't waste any time on self-pity or doubt. Throw yourself into the next project." I don't go so far as to suggest that my goal is to get upstream and spawn. I also understand that the word "determination" is not quite right to describe a fish, and that van Gogh wasn't driven by mere instinct. But—at least for today—the herring join van Gogh as my role models.

Outside my window the gray soup sea rises over the jetties. I hunch down to my work. I could be wrong about my writing. I could be deluding myself; there's no evidence to the contrary. But because I don't see any other choice, I just keep going, as if it's something I am meant to do. And maybe it is. "Don't worry too much about consequences," I write in my journal. "Just keep throwing yourself into things. And think like a herring."

JUNE

❧

June 1

Arun and later a walk around the neck. The smell of freshly cut grass and honeysuckle. A bobwhite with chestnut brown underside. The white underbands of a mockingbird. A catbird singing, "like a parakeet," as my mother would say. The two constants of this place—the birds and the soughing of the wind through the leaves.

The Cape evenings overwhelm me. This time of year is a blessing, a gift. The excess of nature—it has so much to give, to spare. Tomorrow my father arrives. He'll be far away from his doctors, the hospital here isn't great, and this house wasn't built for a sick man. Still, we're all convinced that this is the right place for him to come.

June 3

At 4:45 I came sounding up from sleep. The rain was steady then. It continues. Sometimes a gentle layered tapping. Right now thick drops plopping on the tar shingles of the roof. A mourning dove's hollow song cuts through the rain. The house, musty.

It's still raining when they arrive at three. I've been warned, but am shocked when I see him. The second round of chemo has been unkind. Thin and wrinkled, his neck strains forward like a mud turtle's and his blue eyes shine out against pale skin. Alone in the kitchen with my mother, she tells me a story. In the hospital a few days before, he had "bitched at" her in front of a nurse. As the nurse wheeled him away, she leaned over and said to my father, "You should be nicer to your daughter. She's so understanding."

Still, if he doesn't look like my father, he still sounds like him. He points at the weeds on the back patio with his cane: "We'll pull those up tomorrow." Then the cane shoots out toward the ivy: "We'll rip some of that down, too." I thought I'd gotten the house in great shape, but he lets me know otherwise. "We'll fix it all up over the next months," he says. "It'll mean big, big bucks down the line."

June 4

I become a day laborer. "Life is maintenance," my father tells me again. Maintenance is his dying theme and he plays it fortissimo. I spend the morning cutting a lawn that has just been cut. I wonder if it wouldn't be equally helpful to leave the mower running outside his window, soothing him with its song of labor. Signs of industry and organization reassure him. As if to die in a neat, well-trimmed house will make all the difference.

"Ready for your first inspection?" he asks. He comes out, points and jabs with the cane. "This should be yanked," he says, gesturing at a clump of weeds. He limps over to the side of the house, where the trash waits to be picked up. "It looks like a goddamn trailer park," he grouses.

Unable to control his cells, he tries to control what he can. Anything shaggy or overgrown is bad. It makes me want to own a house where I never cut the lawn, leaving it unkempt and spotted with thistle and dandelions. It would be no use. His ghost would sneak back to clip and prune in the middle of the night.

It's unfortunate that dying won't conform to his schedules. At least when he dies he'll finally be "organized." He knows I'll be sure to weed his grave.

While I have some complaints about his style, I find him remarkable. He rarely complains about the pain, works on selling his business and on his will—"getting things organized for your mother"—and loses himself in conversation as the endless parade of friends streams through the house. If he wants the weeds pulled, so be it.

June 5

Found a dead seal on the beach today. Its body was about three feet long, black, vaguely spotted. It had claws for toenails and the whole carcass was entwined in brown-purple seaweed and yellow beach grass. The head, its flesh apparently chewed off, stared up at me. The vertebrae of the neck were completely exposed. I cringed when I first saw it, grabbing at my own neck to make sure everything was in place.

My mother looks frail, a word I never thought I'd use to describe her. Too many shocks, too many jolts. She hunches over her cigarettes. "She's the only woman in the world who responds to her husband having lung cancer by starting to smoke again," says my father.

I dream about her falling sick, too, but it's a possibility I don't even want to consider.

June 6
National Cancer Survivor's Day

Last night Mom filled in more details about my father's toxic reaction to the second round of chemo. The drugs poisoned his system and he essentially went crazy for three days. His hospital room began to spin, golf balls flew out of the TV screen, extension cords slithered into figure eights, and gremlins communicated to him by pointing thumbtacks on the bulletin board in different directions. Unraveling his hospital blanket became his main goal. "I've got a good one here," he'd say if he found a thread he could pull apart. Once, on the way back from the bathroom, he snuck his fingernail scissors out of his mess kit and hid them so he could cut into the blanket's edge when he was alone. But his diabolical smile gave him away. "What did you do now?" my sister asked. Sheepishly, he showed her the scissors. As she took them away he shrugged and smiled. "Can't blame a guy for trying," he said.

My sister was both terrified and hard-pressed not to laugh. "He was tripping his brains out," she later told me over the phone.

My father laughs about this episode, too, but he must hate the thought of it. Of losing control. Of his mind, usually such a sharp and discerning machine, suddenly going haywire. "Nothing is private in the hospital," he said in a trembly voice. "You lose all privacy and self-respect."

~

Hiking up to Stone's bluff, I picture Lear raging on the heath during the storm. The comparison makes sense to me. Both men, kings of their worlds, had things "under control" from a young age. My father went to Harvard Business School and was president of his company by the time he was thirty. What's it like to have it all suddenly come undone? Like Lear he's had his cosmology unraveled. Not betrayed by daughters, but by cells.

By the end of the play, Lear, in jail with Cordelia, had earned gentleness and compassion through his trials. My father now speaks in a soft voice. The hair on the side of his head is so thin and light that you want to stroke it, take care of him. The lion is going out like a lamb. He seems so much gentler, so much more sympathizing and sympathetic.

Unfortunately, there is another similarity between his story and Lear's. That would be the ending. And that ending angers me.

I hear Lear rage in my head.

> Blow, winds, and crack your cheeks! rage! blow!
> You cataracts and hurricanoes, spout
> Till you have drenched our steeples, drowned the cocks.

Then, walking along the bluff, I take the opportunity to do some raging of my own. My anger is decidedly less articulate.

"Why?" I yell at the sickly green ocean. "Why the fuck?" Melodramas call for the melodramatic. Yelling does some good.

Feeling jittery, overcaffeinated. Worried about sickness claiming the other members of my family, I can't sleep. I take a night walk. Staring up at branches reflected against the front of the house, caught in the beam of the spotlight. Jagged crosshatching. A reflection like barbed wire shaken by an unseen hand.

I walk up the street away from the house. An indigo sky swollen with clouds, dark and troubled at the center, white and clean along the edge. A strange map of an unknown country.

In the distance, a sudden, jerky movement. I can barely make it out. It stands perfectly still, attempting to blend in with its surroundings. It's tall, taller than a man, with a pale, almost luminescent face. I am terrified. Should I run away? Despite my fear, I move forward. Crouched, ready to fight, I angle in and, finally, make out the shape in the moonlight. I laugh out loud. I have met my enemy and it is a street sign. There it stands, tall and white.

"No Parking This Side," it says.

So many good friends. Many nights we eat at different friends' homes, despite the fact that my father is so tired. Usually he gets swept up in the festivity, becomes animated, involved, telling funny anecdotes, invariably getting the biggest laughs of the evening.

Last night we ate at Heidi Schadt's. She seems perfectly suited to dealing with the situation. People talk about not knowing how to act or what to do, and most people really don't. Heidi knows. She knows people try to live as they have lived. That the nourishing things—food and drink and sleep and friends—are the most important. She brings by a bowl of potato salad, stocks us with toothpaste, detergent, and Spray and Wash, helps clean the house. She knows we try to live day-to-day, knows we do this not because it says to in some self-help book about dealing with grief, but because it's how we live anyway, all of us.

We had a fine dinner, punctuated with Heidi's loud *ha-ha*s and lots of wine. My father looked good.

June 10

The wind is constant, rippling through the post oak and pines, moving through them all morning like waves. Here the wind actually whistles.

My life would make Robert Bly do cartwheels. In just a few short years I have lost my mythic golden ball and now am losing my father. As for Bly's movement, the idea of men sweating together and beating drums is trendily nauseating. An easier solution would be just to keep playing sports. Playing sports all these years has given me everything the men's movement supposedly wants—an arena in which to be a hero, a group of male (and female) friends who sweat, talk, play, and drink together. Intentionally or not, Bly has taken a real thing and made it seem cheesy. He's done for manhood what McDonald's did for hamburgers.

Still, he asks some valid questions. Like, How do we live without fathers? Without someone to show us how to be?

This morning that someone looks like a prison-camp survivor as he emerges from the bathroom. For a man who always took up so much space suddenly to be emaciated! His body is thin and freckled, very much a bag of bones.

I'm impressed that he still walks around the house in just his boxers. I admired his lack of self-consciousness when he was too fat and I admire it now that he's too thin. The rest of us—my mother included—are vain. The whole family fell to the fitness bug long ago. We worry about pinches of fat, and take off our clothes in proportion to how good we feel about our bodies. I think it's fair to say that I'm the most vain, and like to strut around shirtless when I'm feeling strong. But my father struts, or lumbers, no matter his shape. It's his house and he will greet guests in boxers if he chooses.

And as *his* shape deteriorates, *I* work out fanatically. Fear is a wonderful motivator.

June 12

"Cancer books don't sell," an agent told me the other day. I wonder whether he's right, and, if so, why. There is the obvious answer that we don't want to hear about it. But since one out of three families is affected you'd think plenty of people would be curious. I think disease is the modern adventure, the one almost all of us face.

June 13

Another rainy morning, the smell of oil paint rising off my sister's paintings. My father's mania for order is contagious. Up here in my study I suddenly find myself making notes, checking boxes, planning.

He sits at his card table on the deck below me. He is leaning, sifting. He stacks empty beers for the recycling man, moving cans of Miller Lite delicately, as if they were chess pieces. As he works he breathes heavily, talks to the cans—"Come on, guys," he says to the obstinate ones—sniffles and snorts. Whether he's keeping himself alive or killing himself by doing these things is open to debate.

I see him try to drag a lawn chair across the porch. I jump up and run downstairs to help him.

Is this all there is in life? Is this what it's all about?

Control. Is it as large an issue for everyone as we make it in our family? He is angry at his cancer. It's not at all under his control. And so he needs to control what he can. Dishes in the right place, cans organized, etc.

"Writing is breaking the illusion of control." This from the mother, a writer, of one of my students. Is it true? Or is writing also a way of putting things in their place? Metaphysically neatening up cans, organizing the unorganizable flux?

If not the content of writing, then certainly the routine helps give order and the illusion of control to my life. "Good habits are worth being fanatical about," John Irving said. I *must* write every morning, like an athlete who must work out. I might not see my father again after this month, yet I resent the interruptions to my morning routine. How can I write when I'm constantly bringing him Pepsi, taking him Percocet, emptying the trash when he urgently wants it emptied, feeling guilty when I'm not near him? It sounds—it *is*—remarkably selfish, but I'm less of a person, less able to deal with him, if I don't write first.

June 16

Last night more cancer dreams. Now everyone in my family has died at least once in my subconscious.

My father and I share a fascination with birds. I might know their names a little better, but take no greater delight. This morning goldfinches, a brilliant scarlet tanager, a downy woodpecker, and a drab female cardinal with a candy-corn beak. I wish he could come to the beach with me one morning to see the swallows putting on their show. White bellies and split tails. Fluttering, swooping, then hanging in the wind. They burrow into the rich red-clay sand directly below the bluff's hairy-tufted top, and fly and dart, seeming to dive right into the cliffside before pulling up short and landing lightly at their own dirt doorsteps. Yesterday I counted twenty-six of their holes along the top of the bluff wall.

Sometimes he enjoys watching birds in a purely sporting manner. He loves to see his cats stalk them. "In nature you only have to lose one step and—*whommpf*—someone gets you." He shoots out his hand to demonstrate. He talks about an old cat of his, a great hunter, Mr. Kitty. He points to the three finches now hovering around the feeder.

"Mr. Kitty would have had all of them for lunch. *Swipe-swipe-swipe.*" He shoots his hand out three times.

June 17

The mining of joy. That would be a good line of work. Is it still possible to travel some of the same paths the Romantics did? Why not? Our brains are the same. Not to experience God per se in an oak tree, but to experience something miraculous, delightful. To open up those pathways now considered the sole realm of drugs. To "go negative" as Whitman did. To resist, like Thoreau, following the same tired, tamped paths in the brain.

I remember the evening I spent at Walter Jackson Bate's farmhouse in New Hampshire. I asked him if he believed in God.

"Oh, yes, I suppose," he said. He pointed out through the plate-glass window. Rain poured down hard on the flower beds and mist rose above the hills. "I have to believe there is something behind such a miraculous world."

His statement surprised me, but not as much as the adamancy of my own response.

"I can't belive in Heaven," I said. "Heaven seems the worst case of wishful thinking. Like believing in Santa Claus."

He looked at me carefully.

"I said I believed in a God who created the universe," he said. "I never said I believed in the afterlife."

June 20

I lie by the water, listening to its steady breathing. Lapping the shore, then sliding sibilantly outward. I let the third beer settle in my stomach, the sun burning my belly to a crisp. The heat comes from below as well, up from the sand, spreading through my body. Today, in many ways, is the most beautiful yet. The temperature and low humidity are perfect. For my health I take the waters. The sun cuts an angle straight toward me and I dive into the bracing gold. I splash the salt on my face, listen to the waves' gruff mantra. At times like these it seems as if the Cape is helping me deal with my father's sickness. Like an old friend, helping me cope.

I'm taking a nap at the house when my parents return from the boat ride. My mother comes home first and her sobbing wakes me. It's a sound infrequently heard in this house. I go downstairs and hold her while she lets go.

"It's just so awful, so awful," she says as her body convulses. "It was so beautiful out on the bay. And we were there with our friends. It was just like it used to be. But it isn't like it used to be. *He's so sick.*"

She can't stop and when she heads to the bathroom I start to lose it. Until he walks in. Then I pull myself together, get him his little pillows, set him up in his chair.

Why is it that the only time I'm able really to *feel* is when my mother breaks down? Even then, I'm distant. Look at me now— writing in here as she continues to cry out on the back deck.

Why do you write?

I've heard so many pompous answers to that question. I write to be like my father. To get organized—to put things in their place.

June 23

My mother harasses him about taking his afternoon nap. "I'll have plenty of time to rest soon enough," he barks, then lets go with a low, loud chortle.

As they head out to see the plots at the Quivet cemetery, he yells: "We're off to see the final resting place, David." I hear his trailing laughter as the door slams.

I was the same way with my cancer. The fact that it hit me in the balls was all the more reason to joke. But I don't feel like laughing anymore. My father ages before my eyes. I witness the slow, elderly movements, the methodical double-checking, the painful wincing. Later in the day he's an old white spider bent over his bed, sitting there without moving, just thinking. But thinking about what?

June 24

A low line of blue-gray clouds moves quickly from left to right. A smaller, whiter group, all bunched up, floats higher and more slowly in the opposite direction. The two groups create a dying, shifting light. The post oak is illuminated, radiant.

Today my mother looks exhausted, at times almost haggard. Strange to see this endlessly optimistic and energetic person so drained. Still, I know she will boost herself back up soon. She needs to help him.

How much human beings must put up with.

My parents will leave in a couple of days. I keep waiting for a wrap-up speech from him, perhaps expecting him to reveal the meaning of life. At this point I wouldn't be surprised if he knew it. But despite his aggressive nature, he's never really been big on counseling me. My whole life, I've rebelled against imagined advice.

About as close as he comes to a wrap-up is telling me not to misplace his tools while he's gone.

"You leave something one way, you want to find it that way," he says. "Someday you'll understand."

From Tom Clark's biography of Charles Olson:

Reading Pound's prose, he [Olson] felt at once challenged, intimidated, provoked and awed. In his journals, Pound had already become a princi-pal sparring partner, pervading his mind with a shadow presence that went well beyond mere influence. "Should you not best him?" he goaded himself. "Is this form not inevitable enough to be used as your own? Let yourself be derivative for a bit. . . . Write as the fathers to be the father."

June 26

This morning my mother chastised him when he tried to empty the trash.

"I'm keeping my mind occupied," he snapped.

Lounging in the hammock, I watch the chickadees gorge at the feeder. We gave the hammock to my father five years ago, for his fifty-second birthday. I've watched him sand it, paint it (with two coats, of course), assemble it, disassemble it, drag it down to the cellar to store for winter, drag it back up for summer. But I don't think I've ever seen him lie in it.

Still, I think it was a fine gift, occupying his mind as it did.

Sammy Mack now owns a limousine service. He's offered to give my father a ride to Logan Airport for free, doorway to doorway. This is typical of the way our friends and acquaintances have ral-lied around him. It reminds me a bit of the communal spirit on the Cape when hurricanes threaten. Everyone nailing up ply-wood, helping pull each other's boats, rushing about in the gen-eral sense of panic, and, yes, excitement. These were the most ex-citing times here when I was a kid. Sneaking down to the beach to watch the storm sweep in. Jumping off the dunes with my coat open and actually flying for a few short feet.

June 27

When he left I tried to be affectionate. I squeezed his shoulder as I said goodbye and accidentally pinched his cancerous lymph node. He winced and cried out in pain. "Jesus," he yelled.

June 28

Sunlight ripples off smooth humps of water. The ocean is even warmer after the storm. The beach is strewn with weeds, jellyfish, clumps of kelp. Seagulls bark like marine sergeants.

Rode my bike out to Paine's Creek. Parked at the landing and ogled a young brunette in black leotards and purple cutoffs. Swam in the little cove—the water bathtub warm. The backs of mating horseshoe crabs were covered with periwinkles, green sea grass, and barnacles like golden rust. Are there crustier characters anywhere?

It's time for me to leave this house. I have lived in my father's house for too long.

June 29

Today all the lines and cleats, everything that isn't tied down, are dinging against the masts and flagpoles. Another sound, which I can't place, comes from the harbor. A sound like the shaking of a huge aluminum sheet.

I walk down to the harbor, then toward the beach. Black, wet phone lines bounce up and down, and the gray phone box sizzles. At the beach, debris has been kicked up by the storm. Clumps of beach stalks and hundreds of black skate eggs. Horseshoe crab shells—brown, black, and one golden brown—crunch underfoot. A blue-capped milk carton, an empty bag of cottage fries, and a can of motor oil under the sea stairs.

On the way home I pass the plywood husk of a new house. Piles of red cedar shingles, stacked in large bundles by the front door, smell good enough to eat. They vary in size: some are only about half a hand's span wide, others—the ones that my old boss Gus called bedsheets—seem to cover whole walls. I've both stapled and nailed shingles. Either way, they're attached to a house in an uneven pattern, overlapped like bricks. The edges of the row on top are never allowed to line up with the edges of the row below, otherwise water would seep in. Today the shingles are an orange-gold, but after a few years of the wind's brackish assault, they will darken and take on their strange gray character.

My walks keep me sane.

July 2
Dad's birthday

"Death is a matter of style," said Antole Broyard. I wouldn't choose my father's style; I define myself against him. At times he lives as if pruning were the highest function of mankind. Life is mowing and fixing and scraping and planning, planning, planning. Yet there is something tremendously heroic about all this. He continues to fight his fight in the face of death.

And, of course, all this fussing can't hide how much he cares about all of us. "To my family," he toasted the night before he left here. "Who could ask for more?" He broke down and couldn't stop crying.

The letters of appreciation keep pouring in. Sarah, the ex-mayor of Worcester, writes

you were the dearest and closest friend that Gavin and I had in our marriage. . . . Your irascibility is only exceeded by your desire for no one to know what a Teddy Bear you can be. Your caustic sense of humor is only exceeded by your thoughtful concern for your friends—to the point of unilaterally finding solutions to others' problems. You are the epitome of a fun-loving genius. You are a tender and treasured friend and always will be.

I wrote my own letter to him for his birthday. In it I detailed all the gifts he has given me—gifts of persistence, delight, humor, concern.

How do we live in the face of death? Broyard was still writing *Intoxicated by My Illness* when he died. In it he quotes Brunner's *The Denial of Death*. The way to fight death is "by becoming so insistently ourselves." Certainly my father has done this, and by doing so has provided me with a role model for both living and dying. The lesson he teaches me is not to be like him, but to be insistently like myself.

To be heroic is our deepest wish. I feel a sharp pain in my shoulders and fear my own death again; cancer is closing in like the tide. Probably this is hypochondria. Or paranoia. No matter. The solution is the same either way: to live heroically. How? It means different things for different people. For me, it means to throw myself into writing. To love my friends and family. To keep strong physically and live like an athlete. To have some physical connection to place.

And to live this way *insistently*.

FOLLOWING THOREAU

✧

"**O**h, you're doing the Thoreau thing?"
He is a plump little man, balding, with small patches of orange hair. He works as a ranger at the Cape Cod National Seashore, but from the looks of him he never gets out from behind his desk. He asks his question dismissingly, with an air of superiority.

Yes, I admit, I want to follow Thoreau's route up the outside of the Cape. Doing the Thoreau thing makes it sound like some sort of dance, and the idea of the hike, which I thought so original just a minute ago, now seems tired. I picture hordes of us, Thoreau wannabes—individualists all—marching out over the dunes.

"It's a hard walk, you know."

He says this sternly and looks me up and down, deciding whether or not I'm up to it. That's better. Maybe I imagined the condescension. I lift up my backpack and assure him that I've done a good deal of camping in the West. He nods and helps me plot the trip on my map. By the time I leave he seems genuinely interested in my journey. He points me out to a fellow ranger.

"This guy's going to do the Thoreau trip," he brags.

Well, not exactly. Thoreau started his journey in Concord. I plan to hike from Eastham to Provincetown, taking three days as Thoreau did. Henry called it a "leisurely walk." We'll see.

I began following Thoreau seventeen years ago as a sophomore in Dianne Meade's English class. We read the transcendentalists during the third week of school, and, while the rest of the class moved on, I got caught on a snag named Henry. I'm not really sure how Thoreau gets a hold on so many of us: sometimes his language seems as stilted as old English, but there's something that starts us tearing through his pages. Thinking I'd made an entirely original discovery, I never suspected that mine was an archetypal, even clichéd, awakening. I began reading *Walden* and, before I knew it, was starting a journal of my own; next I discovered the town woods, began to dream about being a writer, and wondered why I spent so much time working at football and getting good grades.

I hope the schools never stop teaching *Walden* to fifteen- and sixteen-year-olds. It's the right time for it. Joyce Carol Oates writes:

> it is the *Walden* of my adolescence that I remember most vividly—suffused with the powerfully, intense romantic energies of adolescence, the sense that life is boundless, experimental, provisionary, ever-fluid and unpredictable; the conviction that, whatever the accident of outer self, the truest self is inward, secret, inviolable.

Walden also dovetails nicely with the adolescent's instinct for rebellion. I had a father who responded to a grade of ninety-seven on a test by asking, only half-joking, "What about the other three points?" Part of Thoreau's appeal was a voice every bit as strong and authoritative as my father's, but with a wholly different message.

"The life that men praise and call successful is but one kind," he preached.

"Amen," I yelled back.

I like myself best when I'm hiking. This I think as I churn up the beach. A romantic thought, of course. Really what I'm doing is somewhat repetitive and painful—carrying a backpack through deep sand as the straps cut into my shoulders, looking out at a scene of beach and ocean I've seen a thousand times before. But I'm happy, stupidly so, for whatever reason.

While some parts of the Cape have filled up with Dairy Queens and 7–11s, here there are no stores and few houses. Like Thoreau, I stick to the "backside of the Cape." On my left loom cliffs of sand with red clay streaks, to my right lies the Atlantic. It doesn't take long to realize the advantage of taking my shoes off and hiking close to the water, where the sand is hard and more firm. I try to avoid the orange blotches of jellyfish that dot the shore. It's an uneven sort of hike—one leg up higher than the other—not a "tramp-tramp" but more a "tramp-sludge-tramp-sludge," like a soldier with a wounded leg.

The waves set a cadence for my march. That's the paradox here; the constancy of the waves and the flux of the shore, water constantly sculpting land. After a while I hike up closer to the dunes and walk through the kelp beds, hundreds of black flies shooting off before my steps. The beach's yard sale is full today: an old laundry basket, detergent jugs, chunks of green Styrofoam, a trash can, a tangled green net, and dozens of pieces of driftwood twisted in dead-steer shapes.

It turns out that by walking closer to the dunes I intrude on another's turf. Terns, nesting nearby, go on the alert. They ward me off, circling, screeching, making a show of it, while their offspring scoot behind them, no bigger than plovers. The terns are wonderful fliers, with sleek bullet bodies like living check marks and swallow-type wings. Even running they're aerodynamic, tucking their heads low like bike racers.

I see human fauna, too. A band of surfers lying on the beach in black wet suits look like a gathering of seals. In their midst is one girl in cutoff dungarees and a black bikini top. The top pushes her breasts up and in, a white rim of flesh circumnavigating the black. I feel my shoulders go back and my pace quicken, moving with stronger strides until the group is far behind.

It's a clear day in late spring and I walk without a shirt though I know I'll burn. I read recently in one of my father's cancer books that lying out in the sun is like lying beside a nuclear reactor. But while the scientists tell us the sun is our enemy, I can't help holding on to older, healthier associations. Two Junes ago I had daily doses of another kind of radiation. After treatment I felt like I was driving around on the back of a bus drinking cheap beer—extreme nausea the entire month. I insist that this, the sun's radiation, is different. It makes me feel whole, healthy, full.

I've found my rhythm now. Chomping a carrot, enjoying the mindless physical exertion, breathing in and out to the beat of the waves. What a joyful thing locomotion can be! Though I swore I would take a three-day vacation from worrying about him, I find myself thinking about my father. He can no longer feel the simple physical pleasure of moving, of swinging his arms and walking and breathing without pain. I walk for him, too.

Joseph Wood Krutch wrote of Thoreau's "purely instinctive delight in physical activity" and of "an instinctive, primitive, perhaps animal, delight in bodily functioning."

It was this Thoreau who affected me most in my early twenties. My copy of *Walden* was black and squat, and looked, appropriately enough, like a well-worn Bible. Over the years, since high school, it had been battered. It was dog-eared and well-pawed, held together by white athletic tape—I worried I'd tear it to pieces. The markings were emphatic; they'd left deep grooves and troughs below many of the sentences. When I skimmed the book, I'd run my fingers over the back sides of these indentions. They rose out of the page like hummocks, traveling across in planted rows. They felt uneven and pleasant on my fingertips. I would close my eyes and read the rows like Braille.

I remember hunching down low over the book. I sat next to the wood stove in my mother's spindly black rocking chair but didn't rock. I leaned forward heavily, elbows on knees. Every once in a while I muttered "fabulous" and stabbed my pen at the book. One passage elicited a particularly violent stabbing. I read aloud:

As I came home through the woods with my string of fish, trailing my pole, it being quite dark, I caught a glimpse of a woodchuck stealing across my path, and felt a strange thrill of savage delight, and was strongly tempted to seize and devour him raw; not that I was hungry, except for the wildness which he represented.

I looked up from the book. "Savage delight," I said out loud. "Fabulous."

Later that day, coming back from the beach, I spotted a rabbit. The rabbit twitched its nose, sensed me, froze. I padded quietly up behind an old, deeply carved locust tree. While the rabbit stared out with its black eyes and tapped its foot nervously, I readied my weapon. I curled my fingers around the sandy, dog-chewed plastic. I crouched like an Indian; my eyes bored into the gray-and-black-speckled pelt as I screwed myself up into a tight knot. Ten, fifteen seconds passed. I tensed my body. Then, with an abrupt, violent jerk, I sent the Frisbee spinning toward its warm-blooded target.

I wonder what I would have done with a rabbit corpse. Eaten it raw? Cooked it on a spit? Charged at it and sunk my teeth into its furry neck? Fortunately the Frisbee missed, or I'd likely have broken into a fit of blubbering apology, hugging the poor creature to my chest and blurting "sorry" after "sorry." Of course, I was really plagiarizing, not hunting. By day I read of Thoreau's urge to mug a woodchuck. By night I tried to murder rabbits.

~

I hike up at Cahoon Hollow Beach. At first the trees are stunted, just as Thoreau described, but as I walk inland, by Great Pond, they grow taller, much taller than any he wrote of. The Cape of today looks more like it did two hundred years before Thoreau than like Thoreau's Cape. When the Pilgrims arrived they spoke of the fine soil and varied woods, but Henry saw a much more barren land, spotted occasionally with "scrubby wood." The Cape was one of America's first and most graphic examples of industry destroying an environment. Those industries were shipbuilding and the salt works—huge wooden vats where salt was gathered when seawater evaporated. Together they stripped the land of trees.

Thoreau called my town, Dennis, "exceedingly barren and desolate country." These days a wild moat of briars, bayberry, fruit trees, oak, locust, and pine surrounds my house, and it wasn't too long ago I saw the coyote dipping into the bushes below our property. "Yet there were deer here once," Thoreau wrote. Three mornings ago I surprised two deer that had climbed down to the beach at low tide. Despite all the development, in some ways today's Cape is closer to what we consider wild than Thoreau's.

I set up my camp and then cheat a little bit. I walk into Wellfleet to rent a mountain bike. The guy who rents it to me talks excitedly about his plan to move to Colorado and race bikes. I warn him about the altitude.

"I figure it'll take me about a week or two to get used to it," he boasts. *A year or two is more like it,* I think. But if I imagine I know more about riding in the West, I soon find myself ill-suited to his home turf. I've never seen such sandy trails, and get bogged down again and again.

Thoreau would have hated mountain bikers. I've imagined startling him when bombing down single tracks in Concord. He would have sneered or thrown a pinecone. "Americans have no play in our play," he said. I like to think that's changed—our play is the best thing about us—but I doubt he'd agree. Maybe if he kept an open mind he would have found his *instinctive, primitive, perhaps animal, delight* in flying down a hill.

Great Pond lives up to its name. A fine dip and then back to the ocean. As the earth continues its turn and the sun goes down on the other side of the Cape, the beach takes on a different light. A fingernail-clipping moon appears and the colors grow rich; the dunes darken and the breakers flash white and radiant. The kelp is a rich maroon—sand fleas jumping everywhere—and the sea-weed a burnished red. Pieces of driftwood appear more gnarled and twisted in this light, and even a small empty bottle of Lux detergent is lit up, taking on a mystic tint.

I ride back to the campsite through the woods in the dark. My father has reacted to his mortality by seeing life as a giant things-to-do list with death just another box to check off. As death approaches we all become more obsessed with our obsessions. What would obsess me? I'd probably write, but I like to think I'd take a trip similar to this one if I had the energy. When Teddy Roosevelt was in his early twenties, doctors told him that he had a heart problem and would die if he overexerted himself. He responded by initiating a massive program of exercise, and by throwing himself into more and more strenuous adventures. He lifted weights, rode horses, and went West to spend weeks camping and hunting in the Badlands.

Not a bad way to react.

Part of Thoreau's appeal is that his literary mood swings come fast and furious. "I am large, I contain multitudes," bragged Whitman. So, too, Thoreau. Joseph Wood Krutch wrote that "to unite without incongruity things ordinarily thought incongruous *is* the phenomenon called Thoreau." The joy of reading Thoreau is being in the presence of a personality that constantly moves, that dances from railing against the "mass of men" and their institutions to describing his own wild urge to attack a woodchuck to orphic utterances such as his conclusion: "The sun is but a morning star."

Another reason for Thoreau's appeal is his emphatic speech. He wrote of "sentences uttered with your back to the wall," and, indeed, many of his one-liners sound like aggressively defensive responses to unspoken accusations. Why haven't you traveled more? *I have travelled a good deal in Concord.* Why don't you have a wife? *All nature is my bride.* And so on.

Of course, if he *only* had his back to the wall we wouldn't read him. *I fear lest my expression may not be extra-vagant enough, may not wander far enough beyond the narrow limits of my daily experience.* At times his words sound the opposite of defensive—exuberant, playful—and at other times he goes beyond even that, straying into raw brag. In *Walden* he tells us he "will brag as lustily as chanticleer in the morning."

If merely a case of literary bad manners, why is this boasting so uplifting? I think because we find ourselves in the presence of that most rare of creatures, the unrepentantly happy human being. In the end, this becomes one of the most obvious reasons for Thoreau's popularity. In our age of twelve steps and empowerment, *Walden* is the ultimate self-help book. His words seems to hold the secret to happiness. *This life is not for complaint, but for satisfaction.* Krutch believes that whereas most artists search for something they don't have, Thoreau, at Walden, "was a finder rather than seeker," and this accounts for the "magistral confidence" of the book.

Back on the three-day trek, I'm feeling something less than magistral confidence myself. *My spirits rose in proportion to the outward dreariness.* Yesterday I hoped for some bad weather, but today I'm not so sure. As I shake off sleep and emerge from my dome tent the sky darkens, giving my decamping a sense of urgency. I'm uncertain about the water repellence of my borrowed sleeping bag and pack. I jam the tent in its sack, fold up the ground cloth, and pile them on the pack-mule bike. I push the bike back to the rental store, then head east on the road. A burly, bearded guy named Ned gives me a lift back to the beach in his truck. He picked me up, he explains, because he saw my tent. He has worked as a guide for the Appalachian Mountain Club. He spends the ride giving an informal seminar called Hiking Disasters I Have Known.

"I've seen a lot of hairy stuff out there, man," he tells me. "A lot of hairy stuff. Chest pains, concussions, broken ankles. You name it, man."

He drops me off at Cahoon Hollow Beach. I thank him and hurry away. Soon I'm back by the water, legs churning, shoulders aching, staring ahead at a darker version of yesterday's view: the spitting froth of the breakers to my right, orange-spotted jellyfish underfoot, the sea cliffs rising to my left. The cliffs change character as I walk north. They now look like the side of a New Mexico canyon—like orange sandstone—and swallows emerge from their holes high on the walls to dart and dip.

Today the ocean's roar is louder, but still steady. I almost don't want to admit the element of monotony in a beach hike, but my shoulders ache and I find myself taking out my map and planning where I'll have lunch and then dinner. Much lip service is paid to the present moment, but like the rest of us I spend most of my life in the future. "We humans are an elsewhere," writes Reg Saner.

After an hour or so I climb through an opening in the cliffs, emerging at a small pond surrounded by a thick beard of poison ivy. The lip of the cliff provides relief—walking on even, firmer land. I now hike atop what Thoreau called "the backbone of the Cape." A hundred feet above the beach, moving at a giant's pace, I look down at two people-dots below. I think of Maushop, the gentle giant of Wampanoag legend. "In the beginning there was nothing but seawater on top of land," I read in *The Narrow Land*, my book of Cape myths. "Much water, much fog." Not long after that, after Kehtean formed the earth and the people, drowning them once for good measure before re-creating them, Maushop came along. Maushop dug Scargo Lake in Dennis, and formed Martha's Vineyard and Nantucket by emptying the sand out of his moccasins. And it was Maushop who saved the Wampanoag people from the evil bird-monster and who became their great friend and protector. Finally, though, the Pukwudgee—the evil pygmies who lived in the reeds in the marshes—betrayed Maushop. Alone they couldn't defeat him, but together they blinded his sons and finally drove him from the Cape.

Of course, I belabor the obvious by pointing out that pygmies still run the Cape. Instead of giants, more and more of us—smaller and smaller—crowd each other out as we fill up what the Wampanoag called "the narrow land." And the land *is* narrow, far too narrow to hold so many of us, no matter how small.

Few works of literature deal with health and happiness. We know we won't find happiness in modern novels—why should we? Bad lives make better drama. We must mine for the secret in nonfiction, and this, in good part, is what keeps us digging back into *Walden*. In the end the reason is simple. We want to find out what makes Thoreau so happy. Why? Because we want to be happy, too.

According to legend, Maushop's uneasy sleep during the hot months of summer formed the dunes and hollows over which I walk. I follow a brown line of sand that squiggles through a gnarled forest of rich green, retracing a raccoon's handprints, beach grass tickling my shins and knees, the ground cover consisting of yellow hudsonia flowers. Ahead bulwarks and hummocks jut in profile toward the sea. To my left, tucked in the bayberry, poison ivy, and scrub oak, stands an occasional house. Happily, none of the houses rise above the dwarf forest, but settle in contentedly, half hidden.

Modesty and common sense are the essential facts of the best Cape architecture. Faced with wind and water, most Cape Codders built—and build—their houses low, the opposite of skyscrapers. Thoreau wrote:

> Generally, the old fashioned houses on the Cape look more comfortable, as well as picturesque, than the modern and more pretending ones, which are less in harmony in the scenery, and less firmly planted.

Planted. These houses, the best of them, grow out of their landscape, evolving organically. The word "organic" has been claimed and cheapened by the New Agers and hippies, but it fits these houses perfectly. "Organic" is a good word that must be reclaimed; it describes well how the best things—books, houses, paintings—grow out of their surroundings.

Below the ledge where I walk juts an occasional subledge, pockets of sand like crow's nests ten feet beneath me but still almost a hundred feet above the beach. It would be easy to climb down into one of these pockets and live for a while. In one I see a charred fire that stirs my imagination. Maybe I will camp here for the night, or, better, live here for a year.

Why do certain places, certain homes, excite us? The tent or teepee, the tree house or cave. The hidden cottage all our own, sketched in our minds in fuzzy pastels and rich greens. This, too, of course, is part of Thoreau's appeal. The archetypal cabin in the woods. In Provincetown, my destination, there once lived another semisolitary writer, the "dune poet," Harry Kemp. Kemp was an "amateur fighter, hobo, and vagabond poet," who lived in a small, half-buried shack in the dunes outside P-town, a shack even smaller than Thoreau's cabin.

I've read a little of Kemp's poetry, and find his house more interesting than his words. It was built entirely from driftwood, except for a roof covered by tar paper and an uneven chimney pipe held up by three crooked wires. Inside, a small nook of shelter protected Kemp from sand and wind. He filled the space with books, a typewriter, a small cot, an oil lamp, a stove, and a few suits and ties. I like to picture him in there, nestled and typing away, while the sand whipped round outside, stinging the sides of his shack.

I decide that later in the summer I'll spend a week in one of these sand alcoves and have the swallows as my downstairs neighbors. As if on cue, a bird darts out from below, its rich blue back and white underbelly flashing before me.

The rain starts in earnest around ten-thirty, lashing. Like Henry David I now have an aft wind. Thunder rumbles behind the cliffs, black shreds of clouds fly out to sea. The sea is green, a darker black-green where it mirrors the clouds above. A plover whips by and gets shot, windblown, bulleting out over the water. At first the weather stimulates me, but before long I take an older view of nature. Nature as threat, not escape. The lightning strikes closer and the rain soaks me. My worries about the backpack come true—it isn't waterproof.

I line the pack with a garbage bag but still worry that my journal will get soaked. *Then the trip will be wasted,* I think. This absurd thought nicely points out the doubly self-conscious aspect of my journey. Not only do I follow Thoreau and read his account, but I also take notes as I go and have already begun writing my own essay about the trip in my head.

I'm terminally self-conscious and twice removed. How infrequently reality breaks through the grids I build in my mind. Before

I saw my father again I thought I had "placed" him and his tragedy; that, having cordoned his sickness off in one part of my mind, I could handle it, make sense of it. But seeing him the other morning in his boxers—emaciated, boney, flesh sagging—destroyed the grids, at least for the moment. Here was reality—the thing itself.

The lightning is real, too, and it does a fine job of clearing my head. I decide that the safest place to walk is away from the water, under the bluff. This means trudging through deeper sand. I put my head down and work through it, heavy and wet, as the thunder echoes against the cliff and the lightning closes in.

Three hours later, when the rain stops, I breathe a sigh of relief. In a second I go from feeling tiny and terrified in the face of nature's threat to feeling large and exhilarated, full of myself, when the danger passes. Ego floods back in. I want to climb the cliff, my feet astride the Cape like Maushop.

I pass another sign of nature's old might. A house sits precariously close to the edge of the cliff, its walkway dangling down the cliff front, as if someone had just gone sprawling in a tragicomic fall. But even this is a relatively minor sort of destruction—the sea can do much worse. We sometimes forget. In two hundred years we've gone from fearing to romanticizing the wild, as always most appreciating what's nearly lost.

Thoreau's generation saw this swing in perception gain momentum. It was a flowering of the romantic, at times precious, view of nature. But Thoreau's way of looking at nature evolved far beyond the romantic, anticipating our own modern evolution. While Emerson gave Thoreau a starting point, it didn't take long for him to abandon the idea of nature as merely symbolic of the human world. This was particularly true when Thoreau left the pastoral and compatible nature of Concord behind. Climbing Mount Katahdin in Maine, he complained of the "inhuman" element in nature. In his recent biography of Thoreau, Robert D. Richardson writes:

> he found the top of Katahdin a cold, misty, utterly primitive place. . . . It was an experience of nature vast, drear, and indifferent to humankind. . . . Up there, nature was not bound to be kind to man. This discovery was a cold Caucasian epiphany for Thoreau.

Thoreau never made it to the peak of Katahdin, turning around when it was easily within his reach.

On Cape Cod, Thoreau also saw an inhuman nature. His trip began with a shipwreck and dead bodies strewn on the shore. *This gentle ocean will toss and tear at the rag of a man's body like the father of mad bulls, and his relatives may be seen seeking the remnants for weeks along the strand.* While it has been quoted before, most recently in Robert Finch's introduction to *Cape Cod*, it's important to print in full the passage that best sums up Thoreau's particular vision of the Cape's nature:

It is a wild, rank place, and there is no flattery in it. Strewn with crabs, horse-shoes, and razor clams, and whatever the sea casts up,—a vast morgue, where famished dogs may range in packs, and crows come daily to glean the pittance which the tide leaves them. The carcasses of men and beasts together lie stately upon its shelf, rotting and bleaching in the sun and waves, and each tide turns them in their beds, and tucks fresh sand under them. There is naked Nature, inhumanly sincere, wasting no thought on man, nibbling at the cliffy shore where gulls wheel amid the spray.

This is a long way from Emerson's docile nature, where flowers find their symbolic match in the human mind—at once a more modern and more ancient vision than the Emersonian one. And it is a *vision*. The later journals are often cited as examples of Thoreau's dwindling creativity, his increasing, almost scientific, gathering of details. But here we have observed fact and detail creating a picture—a sweeping, swirling, frightening, honest picture.

I eat a lunch of gritty Fig Newtons on the deck of the youth hostel. My teeth crunch on sand. The hostel won't open for another week or two, but the door is unlocked. It takes a few minutes of sitting, dripping wet, on the porch, before cultural fears fade and I enter the empty building. I use the bathroom, towel off my hair, read the paper, check the clock. I've made good time—the lightning prodded me. Of course, if I'd really been threatened, I would have broken into one of the homes along the way. And I'd have had my pick—few places have as many abandoned homes as the Cape before summer starts.

After lunch, I walk on. It only drizzles now, but whitecaps further out suggest more weather to come, and the sand still hisses. The beach moves away from me, scythelike, off to my left, suiting a golfer with a hook. After another hour or two I remember I have a Snickers bar in my bag. I sit down on a piece of driftwood and devour the best meal I've had in months.

I cut inland just before the Highland lighthouse, climbing up a steep slope and finding myself in the middle of the golf links. This is a strange, heath-like country, perhaps closer to the Cape Thoreau saw than the one I'm used to. *As for the interior, if the elevated sand-bar in the midst of the ocean can be said to have any interior, it was an exceedingly desolate landscape, with rarely a cultivatable or cultivable field in sight.* A few trees stand amid the yellow, stubbly grass. The fog is thick—my clothes will never dry. I ask directions from an old, oversalted woman in a yellow slicker.

The trees increase as I walk inland. Following the woman's

directions, I cut across a dirt path that winds through a small, twisted, lichen-stained forest. *It was like a thick stuff of worsted or a fleece.* Here the moss has gone wild, giving everything a hoarfrost coat. Hairy tarantula branches reach out from one bush while the pines strike poses like modern dancers.

I stagger into the Head of the Meadows Campground and discover, happily, that it has a dryer. What did John Muir do at the end of the day hiking through the High Sierra when he and the wood around him were both soaking wet? I get change for a five and start the machine.

After my clothes and sleeping bag dry, I walk into North Truro for dinner. Strands of fog float by my face along with the strong smell of the sea—a mix of fish and salt and water, the essence of the Cape. I buy turkey, mayonnaise, Portuguese bread, a beer. When I ask about the weather the cashier says, "Partly cloudy . . . but partly something else." The last cashier who waited on me told the same joke, as if both had been trained at some Cape Cod Institute for Crusty Comic Tellers.

From the phone outside the store I call North Carolina. The news is bad. The latest CT scan shows that the chemo, which drove my father temporarily insane, did nothing to shrink the cancer. He planned to spend the summer up here but he feels weary and talks about the Cape house as being too small, and the walls too thin. The rest of us still hope he'll choose to come here, but this is mere selfishness. He sighs heavily.

"I don't want to move again," he says. "I just want to die right here."

By the end of the call his old self returns. He says he'll try to get up to the Cape and "stick to the game plan." Death may finally stop him from planning, but the threat of death won't.

In the middle of the night a loud crack of thunder wakes me. I sit up in the tent and wonder what my father is doing.

My mother complains that he has become more and more obsessed with details. With his cane he points out unswept coffee grounds or leaves that need to be raked. It's poignant, but frustrating. "I've got a few things I want to get behind me," he says. "Don't you realize that soon *everything* is going to be behind you?" I want to yell. Though he is brave and never breaks down, I wish he wouldn't worry about so many petty details.

I went to the woods because I wished to live deliberately, to front only the essential facts of life, and see if I could not learn what it had to teach, and not, when I came to die, discover that I had not lived. . . . I wanted to live deep and suck out all the marrow of life.

If I were dying I'd want to confront the essential facts of life. Of course the trick is to determine what those essentials are. To my father they may well be raking or sweeping up coffee grounds.

Earlier today I stared up at one section of sea cliff. It looked like a seated giant, Maushop maybe. Its feet of clay, long orange and brown, stretched out before me. From there the bank sloped up to the knees and cut directly inward, forming a flat lap of charcoal gray, then straight up again through the torso and head, finally capped by a shaggy fright wig of beach grass and bayberry. The swallow holes formed the eyes, though admittedly small and beady eyes for a giant.

How's that for anthropomorphism? Stifling my own adolescent urge for gigantism requires constant vigilance. At first I found Thoreau's *Cape Cod* too plain. I wanted the Thoreau of *Walden*—mystically worked up, breaking a sweat while unspooling spiels. "The homeliest facts are always most acceptable to the inquiring mind," Thoreau reminds us. I was soft, needing the mush of mysticism mixed in with my crunchy, homely facts.

And still, stubbornly, I want more. Thoreau didn't simply hold up a fact as if admiring a carburetor. He did something with facts, even when he believed that Nature didn't. He used them to build. *Nothing remarkable was ever accomplished in a prosaic mood.* Our time is overfascinated with facts and sobriety. A hundred and fifty years ago they picked up a thistle and saw the universe. Today we pick it up and see only its pappi.

Meanwhile the the hokey popular movements have appropriated the symbolic. But astrology and tarot cards won't do the trick. "Everything happens for a reason" is as bad as "nothing means anything." We don't need enemy camps, but a fine mix and balance of hard, rude fact and symbol. I mentioned reclaiming the word "organic," and the first order of business should be taking back some other important words—words such as "flow." We need to reestablish meanings. And we need symbols. Not

pure mush, but an interior landscape of our own, rooted in fact
but not hampered by it.

The pleasure of Thoreau is that he saw both things. And that
becomes our challenge, too. To heal the split. To aspire to em-
brace both fact and flight.

The last morning of my walk. Today I skip my reading and blaze
my own trail. Well, maybe "blaze" is too strong a word. On the
way to the beach I decide, on impulse, to start cutting cross-Cape
on the Pilgrim Springs bike path. It feels fine to walk on good old
concrete again, and the scenery is a delightful mix of sea and one
of Henry David's "sylvan retreats." The fog hangs thick. Looking
through the trees I see a soupy gray mix of sea and sky, the hori-
zon line smudged, in some places completely invisible.

While the machine roar of the sea reminds me of its proximity,
the world I walk through is a lush one, filled with ferns and fruit
trees, birch, daisies, Queen Anne's lace and dandelions, butter-
cups and wild roses. The smells of the sea and the orchard, salt
and honeysuckle, mix together. Occasionally the path gives me a
good view back toward the shore, where I can see the profiles of
the hummock heads and cliffs, looking stranger from this angle,
from behind, like mesas and buttes.

Several landscapes lie between me and the sea. After my little
woods comes a moorland of purple-tinted beach heather, then another stand of pitch pines, then, the land dipping like a swallow's
flight, more heather, then, rising again, the backside of the cliffs.

After two miles the bike path ends and I come out on a dirt
road. I take a left and cross Cape Cod. Where I stand the Cape is
so thin that I can hear Route 6 on the other side. I pass Pilgrim
Lake on my right: cattails grow high beside the road and a red-
winged blackbird makes a chuckling noise before letting go with
one high-pitched note. It takes less than seven minutes for me to
traverse the entire width of the Cape.

Here the Cape was once split on the old maps, separating the
land below from the island of the Province Lands. Here you can
best understand why the Wampanoags called the Cape "the Narrow Land," and here is Thoreau's "edge of a continent wasting before the assaults of the ocean." Nowhere else does our existence

on the Cape seem so tenuous. You understand that we live on a spit of land jutting into the sea, unprotected, almost an island, with waves and wind sweeping across it. And you understand the land's malleability, its ever-changing form. This is a low land, a land born of ice, stripped of its hills by the glacial retreat, changing every year, remolded, reshaped like an artist's clay.

Thoreau mentions the town of Billingsgate several times in his book, and every time he does I feel a small tingle of excitement. Billingsgate is now not much more than a sandbar that appears at low tide. As a child, I dug clams there with my family. We would anchor our boat offshore and run off with nets and bags, searching for air holes that signaled clams below. It was great clamming. We would dig and dig—occasionally hitting monster beds—until the tide began creeping slowly back in. At first the water would engulf certain low points, but soon it crossed the entire sand island, swallowing the land faster and faster, dissecting and filling until water completely covered sand. We would run back to the boat in a happy panic.

Of course, our panic was nothing like what the citizenry of Billingsgate had experienced a century before. I remember my father, sitting behind the wheel of our little powerboat and drinking a warm Schlitz, telling us how Billingsgate had once been a town that jutted into Cape Cod Bay. Then one year the tide began to rise higher and higher, before long swallowing the entire place.

The story fascinated me, and I'd try to imagine how a town could sink into the sea. I saw the ocean gradually rising, filling the grocery store, the blacksmith shop; I saw pots and kettles floating on top of the water. Perhaps, not long after the sea rose, children would return to the old town during the in-between tides. They would explore by foot at first, then swim in and out of the old buildings as the tide rose.

This story can also be seen as a cautionary tale for modern Cape Codders. Though it's easy to scoff at the idea of global warming after a long, tough New England winter, the scientists agree that the changes will occur (and that the cold winters themselves are a sign they are occurring). One of the most dramatic results of warming will be the rise in sea level as a result of polar melting. Even the most modest predictions for melting would make my house, at high tide, an island castle surrounded by a salt-water moat. And a rise of seven feet, the high end of Environmental Protection Agency estimates for a hundred years from now, would flood the roads where I live, making Sesuit neck itself an island and leaving only a series of floating highland bumps.

I try to picture it. The Cape, one of the few constants in my life, gone. Submerged. *A drowned continent, all livid and frothing at the nostrils.* Walking out to the tip of Cape Cod, seeing how low-lying and fragile the land is, it's easy to imagine it sinking below the water. Who knows? Maybe soon an older, meaner embodiment of Nature will brush off its sleeves and show what it can do. A grim picture, but a fascinating one. The ocean reclaiming the land, dragging expensive homes down cliff sides, drowning gas stations, washing and sloshing through the stores of Commercial Street.

I dodge cars on Route 6, then cut back to Stott's Crossing, to Route 6-A. Seven minutes to cross back to my own century. Gone are the strange forests and empty beaches of Eastham, Wellfleet, and Truro. In their place a string of white cabins cram together, shoulders scrunched up, looking irritable and harried. Signs of vacancy entice vacationers, inviting *Visa* and *Mastercard*. Old names—such as the Fore 'N Aft Cottages—strive to paste on authenticity.

"A thousand men could not have interrupted the vastness," Thoreau said of the Cape. Could he have imagined ten thousand? A hundred thousand? Henry, I'm sad to be the one to tell you, but the vastness can—and has been—interrupted. Could you have possibly predicted the thousands of cars that herd back and forth across the bridge every Friday and Sunday evening? Could you even have imagined cars, each spitting its weight in poison into the atmosphere? Faster and faster, more and more.

Some things you couldn't have begun to guess. Swimming among used syringes and sewage, for instance. Or all the tumorous homes bulging from your barren Cape. Since your time we've been forced into smaller and smaller plots. When old man Stone moved to East Dennis in the early part of the twentieth century, he bought the entire neck for nothing. Now each tiny plot is worth a fortune. Even as late as 1960 the Cape still felt like a series of frontier towns, and you could have bought our whole neighborhood for the current price of one house. Today I'd need to be a wealthy man to be able to buy a plot considered undersized just thirty years ago.

It's the way of our time. Maushop dies while the pygmies proliferate. I should know, Henry—I speak to you as pygmy to giant. In the same way Stone claimed Sesuit neck, you, in one casually written, posthumously published book—a book far from a masterpiece—laid claim to the entire Cape.

Early men and women are by nature pioneers, and those who come later explore the explored. While older writers claim huge swaths of land, we now go about cultivating our smaller, limited plots. As I sit down to eat lunch and do my daily reading, I find that I have again plagiarized; this morning I crossed the Cape almost exactly where Thoreau did a hundred and forty-seven years ago. I thought I'd chosen my own route this one time, but I followed him despite myself.

This brings home the irony of my entire trip. How do I justify "doing the Thoreau thing?" In following someone who was never a follower, in making an icon of an iconoclast? Why hero-worship a man who counseled men to be their own heroes? I laugh at my convolutions. The very fact of my writing this essay is due to Thoreau, since he practically created the genre in America. But then he didn't write to fit a genre; he wrote and the genre fit him.

I follow the arc of the Cape toward the misty outline of Provincetown, toward the mating call of foghorns. Here the houses look funkier than elsewhere on the Cape, some of the lawns still lush and green. On the other hand, a few of the houses look ready to be submerged at high tide. They have white clamshell driveways that give off a good strong reek, sea grass and ocean for backyards. Instead of church bells, the humming moan of the lighthouse fills the air.

I make my way toward the center of town. At Dodie's I eat breakfast—an enormous blueberry muffin and three cups of coffee. Afterward, I walk to the center of town and take a seat at a bench in front of the town hall. The coffee provides a jittery view of the parade of varied and twisted humanity marching in front of me. Different drummers, indeed. I wish I could say that I feel happy to see people again, but the crowd at first seems small and gnarled, undersized and undernourished like the pitch pines I slept below last night.

Commercial Street has earned its name. The sea salts of Thoreau's time have vanished. In their place march a family of tourists in Final Four T-shirts, a woman with twin dogs that wear matching plaid visors, two gentle, older men with their arms around each other, and a brutish-looking motorcyclist in a striped cutoff shirt who turns out to have a pleasant face when he stops to talk to a neighbor. Next come an androgynous pirate with woman's breasts, a beautiful girl in faded overalls, and a hulking whale-woman working her way down from George's Pizza, laboring and looking out angrily at the world. I watch a little girl with leg braces roll by in her wheelchair, pushing with thin arms. Then a lesbian couple, both in dungaree cutoffs, and a weather-beaten fisherman with one leg too short and a raised black boot.

Here walk the famous mass of men, and while alone we're interesting enough, together we're pretty ugly. The problem lies in the numbers, the mass becoming more and more massive with every year until every street becomes a commercial street, jammed just as full as this one. Of course, it's hard for us to see the change, but plop Thoreau down in 1997 and his eyes would pop.

Over the last forty years the population of the world has doubled: we now number over five billion, and before long it'll be ten. Interesting times lie ahead and, despite all the warnings, we probably won't react until faced with extreme danger. This is our nature—we'll get to the brink of extinction and then cram for the final exam of survival, pulling an all-nighter trying to save eternity. Never has Henry's philosophy of reducing our needs instead of trying to accumulate more and more looked so good. And never have we seemed so far away from it.

The coffee wears off and I feel tired, my nerves jangled. I head down to the beach to get away from people and take a short nap. I should explore Race Point and the dunes to conclude my trip, but I've seen them before and, anyway, I'm sick of following Thoreau.

I stuff his book deep into my pack, eat a soggy pear, close my eyes, and fall asleep on the sand.

What good has it done me to identify so intensely with a figure from our literary past? And what bad? What do we gain from hero worship? Does it cripple us or free us? Or both?

Walter Jackson Bate wrote the best discussion I've read on the subject. In *The Burden of the Past and The English Poet* he discusses how the oppressive presence of past greatness intimidates. It's easy to think of the past as a time when giants roamed the earth and achieved great things, and feel our own smallness in comparison. This legacy, combined with the modern insistence on originality, can paralyze. We're torn in two by the conflict:

> On the one hand, we have the natural human response to great examples that, from childhood on, are viewed as prototypes . . . and then have suddenly blocking it a second injunction: the injunction that you are forbidden to be very closely like these examples.

As Bate argues, in no other area of life are we told we can't learn by emulating. I learned how to throw a ball from watching my father, learned to be a carpenter by copying Carl. But in literature and the arts so much has been done before that there seems nothing left but to divide up our little parcels of specialized property and try at all costs to seem "original." As an antidote to this crippling self-consciousness, Bate offers the idea of boldness:

> The boldness desired involves directly facing up to what we admire and then trying to be like it. . . . It is like the habit of Keats of beginning each large new effort by rereading *Lear* and keeping always close at hand the engraving of Shakespeare he found in the lodging house in the Isle of Wight when he went off to begin *Endymion*.

And so, Henry, over the years I have tried to learn by reading and emulating you. And by following you I've learned lessons of discipline, self-reliance, appreciation of nature, and openmindedness. I've done things I never would have done without you, like taking this trip. For that I thank you.

That said, I'm now thinking that the time has come to remove your picture from the wall above my desk. I'm sick of following you. I'd like to take my next trip to an unfamiliar place I haven't read about, and that I won't write about either. Or, if I do end up writing about it, I'd like to do so without the funhouse mirror reflections of past writers and writings.

I've been too deferential to my own heroes, too afraid to topple statues. Emerson wrote of

meek young men in libraries, believing it is their duty to accept the views which Cicero, which Locke, which Bacon, have given; forgetful that Cicero, Locke, and Bacon were only young men in libraries when they wrote these books.

I've been one of those meek young men. I've been too polite, but now I'm ready for my extended adolescence to end. After all, fatherlessness is a condition we all eventually have to accept, and which I'll know about soon. Time to thank these heroes, Thoreau first and foremost, for what they've given me and then move beyond. Of course, I'll still be following Thoreau. What could be more like him than taking a path of my own?

GOING OUTWARD

❦

Black-tipped gulls drop mussels onto the harbor parking lot. Then swoop down and gobble up the succulent insides.

Up at dawn for a swim, I walk to the bluff and wade out by the point near Todog Rock. A lobster boat streams by. I swim toward the rocks where the cormorants roost—two of them, on separate rocks five feet apart. They spread their wings into the wind to dry, jutting their pterodactyl heads forward, statue still in identical poses like synchronized swimmers. They wait until I'm close, no more than fifteen feet away, then drop off the rocks and begin their awkward takeoffs.

I dry myself and walk back to the house. I put on coffee, filling the pot to its brim. August means high tide for people on Cape Cod. It's high tide in this house, too—everyone is here. But while full, the house has lost its main occupant and will now be haunted by his corpulent ghost. Larger than life. That's what everybody always said he was. But he wasn't.

In his honor, I run the flags up the pole. The American flag, of course, and "Don't Tread on Me." They fly at half-mast.

The hardest part for him was when they took away his future. During my father's last visit to the Duke Medical Center, Dr. Moore could feel the bumps on his liver just by pressing a hand against his skin. The doctor needed no more tests. He recommended discontinuing the chemotherapy.

"What a relief," my mother said. And it was. The chemo had been devastating.

But to my father it wasn't a relief. Up until then he'd been able to imagine he had a chance. A slim chance, but a chance.

"It's getting a little scary now," he admitted on the ride home. "They've changed the game. We're not trying to win anymore. Just kind of waiting."

The new game was called avoiding pain. To play they equipped us with a small morphine pump that looked like a Walkman and

fit in a pouch kept around his waist. The machine pumped ten milligrams of morphine an hour into a mid-line pic catheter that had been inserted in his arm. We pushed a button to pump extra doses—called boluses—every fifteen minutes.

If the new situation terrified my father, it didn't set him back for long. The next day he was at his desk, attacking bills and writing letters. The morphine overwhelmed him by mid morning, and he dozed off in the chair, his head dropping and rising like a driver fighting sleep. I tried to convince him to lie down but he insisted on sitting. It was still morning, after all. He slept holding a newspaper in front of him, now and then unconsciously turning a page.

The habits of a lifetime die hard, but over the next few days the morphine undercut his productivity. The space he organized became smaller—instead of companies and houses, he now reigned over the little bedside table where he kept his urinal and cane. The haze of the drug made him less and less rational, but he still spoke in his habitual vocabulary. "That's a good system, David," he told me when I placed the morphine pump in a drawer next to his bed for the night. "Let's see the plan," he said the next morning. More and more he hated being alone. The following night when I tried to head off to sleep he called me back. "You're not leaving," he said. "We're still getting everything settled."

The house wakes. Water runs through the pipes behind the walls, gurgling and purling—the bowels of the house in action. A soothing noise, one that reminds me of the lapping of the sea against a boat's hull.

I have a higher joy quotient than most people. It's a gift I got from my mother.

Mom is next downstairs. I worry about her, but really she's holding up well. Her many friends comfort and distract her. We drink coffee on the deck and look out at the harbor.

"Are you ready for today?" I ask.

She nods. At fifty-six she still looks youthful. She pulls on a cigarette—she's promised to give them up on Labor Day.

Despite her addiction, I've always thought of her as the image of health. She throws herself into tennis and golf. Her father was a great athlete: he played for the Yankees, won the Florida State Amateur Golf Championship, and played golf until he died, still shooting in the seventies in his seventies. My mother believes she inherited her strength from him.

If my father was the mad Ahab of this house, trying to instill his vision of order as he ripped out roots and mowed the lawn, my mother is our Whitman, loafing on the grass and singing a song of physical pleasure.

Like Whitman, she loves to brag.

"Have I talked to you since my check up?" she asked me once before my father got sick. "My doctor said, 'I can't believe this. You're so healthy. You've got ninety-nine percent good cholesterol, and the blood pressure of a baby.' He's right, you know. I'm as healthy as a goddamn horse."

Hers is a strange sort of bragging—happy and unselfconscious. It makes people like her.

"I know perfectly well my own egotism," said Whitman in *Leaves of Grass*, "of pure American breed, of reckless health." Justin Kaplan wrote of Whitman's celebrating "the single self happy merely to exist, enjoying the 'ecstasy of simple physiological being.'" When I read these lines I think of Mom. Now I can only hope she remains as healthy as her boasts.

My mother and father are both distinctly American, and distinctly different. My father was a builder, a believer in the end, in the finished product. My mother celebrates process. She fishes for moments.

Everyone helped take care of him, but during the last two weeks I became his personal nurse. I had to support him when he walked, help him urinate, put on his clothes, wake with him in the middle of the night, bring him juice and food. I was also, in his mind at least, in charge of the morphine pump. I untangled the cord and explained the numbers that beeped on the screen, which—as the dosage climbed—began to take on mystical import. Sometimes he got disoriented and yelled for me. "I want David," he called out once. "I need David to do this."

While I worked I grumbled about not having any time for myself or my writing. But now I am more proud of those two weeks than anything I have ever done in my life.

Nursing him, I thought of Lear's words during the storm: "Is man no more than this? . . . Thou art the thing itself; unaccommodated man is no more but such a poor, bare, forked animal as thou art."

This describes my father's end perfectly. First a poor, bare, forked animal: his turtlelike neck straining forward, his bald head a golden jaundiced ball, his heavy morphine lids and unreal green-yellow eyes, his freckled sagging chest and arms, his nodules, like deadly acne, on his back and hairless groin. Then the thing itself: wincing pain cutting through the morphine, the most real thing I've ever seen.

Finally, we come full circle. I helped him urinate, shaking driblets of blood into his urinal, cherry red staining the blue of the container.

This last was a constant reminder of what Ernest Becker calls our "creatureliness," and for me it brought home again and again the senselessness of it all—the fact that for all our plans and dreams we are simply creatures that rot.

~

Before my brother and sisters get up, I hop on my bike and ride over to the cemetery. If the bridge that once spanned the harbor still existed—the bridge the clipper-ship workers once crossed—I could walk over to Quivet neck. But since it doesn't I have to ride out to Route 6-A before cutting back.

The little cemetery is beautiful and crowded with familiar names. Just as in life, the Searses dominate this East Dennis neighborhood. Here lie Moody, Barnabash, Seth, and Jacob Sears. In the middle of another Sears cluster lies Asa Shiverick (1816–1894), who started the shipyard next to my house, and Christopher Hall, the cofounder and shipmaster who inspired the naming of a clipper ship. The graveyard is a congregation, and I see more recent familiar names as well. Heidi Schadt's father, Samuel Sears, is buried here, and so is Nancy Devita, the painter who wrote the brochure about the clipper ships.

My father's gravesite lies below a silvery oak tree that splays shadows across the grass. Some of his ashes will be buried here after the service. I never thought I'd be one of those people who talk to graves, but before I can think my lips are moving.

"How can this be, Dad?" I ask the dirt. "It's like a bad joke."

A surge of depression, then I feel happy. Happy for this place, a place to come to remember him. Off to my left I can see the marsh and Quivet Creek. Today the marsh is a strange lime green patched by purple heather, hazy like a Monet. Silver flicks along the tips of the grasses and plays off the water. I walk down closer and listen. The stalks of reeds rustle against each other. The noise sounds like whispering—but a loud whispering.

I wrote him a letter on his fifty-seventh birthday, two weeks before he died. I read it at the funeral.

You know that I am a hypochondriac and a skeptic, and I think that in the middle of the night we share the same fears. But you have faced your illness with such dignity and determination that I will be less frightened from here on. Once again you have been my role model. You have taught me how to die as well as how to live.

It was true. Morphine clouded his mind at the end, but throughout his illness he faced his reality directly.

When I was younger I resented his use of the term "the real world," as if he felt there was only one world which he alone saw clearly, and that other worlds—mine, for instance—weren't valid. But the term, at least the way he used it, does have meaning. It not only refers to a businessman's world of dollars and profits, but also means facing what *is*, honestly and directly without a lot of guff. Johnson said that "truth such as is necessary to the regulation of life, is always to be found where it is honestly sought." My father agreed.

Near the end people around him kept using the words "soul" and "heaven," maybe telling themselves stories with these words to keep from being terrified. But these weren't my father's words or stories, and I'm glad he didn't experience some sort of deathbed conversion. It wouldn't have suited him. It would have contradicted the story of his life.

My father's afterlife was settling the will, selling the company, fixing up the house in North Carolina, making sure that his wife was taken care of and his mother set up in the best possible nursing home. And writing letters to all of his close friends telling them how much he cared for and appreciated them. A practical afterlife for a practical man.

I walk to the end of the graveyard, lean my bike against a stone wall, and head down Sea Street. The street once connected East Dennis and Brewster across the marsh, but was abandoned by both towns some years back. Like so much of the Cape this street has been marked by a literary predecessor, in this case Robert Finch, who named an essay after this road. That doesn't stop me from enjoying the place, however, and, since it's in my father's neighborhood now, I feel some claim to it.

Here the fight between nature and progress has a clear victor. The road is overrun by sumac, Queen Anne's lace, juniper, bayberry, beach plum, and poison ivy, the last already starting to assume its fall colors. Grass and roots and shrubs crack up through the concrete, working in from the sides to close in on a comical yellow dividing line that still fights for order. Reeds twelve feet tall grow like columns up through the road.

I reach the old rusted sign separating Dennis and Brewster. On

impulse I take off my shoes and walk into the marsh, following the sickly trickle of the creek. I walk across bamboo mats of dead grass stalks, occasionally oozing down into the muck. Further out by the blue mosquito boxes the ground is more solid, interwoven with shells. They crackle like broken crockery beneath my feet.

Wampanoag legend has many stories of the Pukwudgees, the evil pygmies who roamed the Cape causing mischief and worse. Legend says they trained will-o'-the-wisps to lure traveling Indians out into the marshes. When the Indians strayed onto the marsh, the devil, Mahtahdou, trapped them in quicksand.

"I would advise every sick person to evolve a style or develop a voice for his or her illness," writes Antole Broyard. My own cancer transformed me into a stand-up comedian. Perhaps I couldn't face soberly the idea of death at thirty and needed to remove myself from the situation. The voice I chose in my novel about my sickness was glib, laughing in the face of death. "To lose a testicle is to lose a friend," read the book's opening line. "I want to do for testicles what Melville did for whales," I crowed on page three.

My father's was a graver illness and required a graver voice.

The more dire the situation, the more chaotic, and, since we can't abide by chaos, we must fashion something out of it. No wonder he spoke about getting organized right up to the very end. Organization was simply the theme he chose; his art to control chaos.

On a primitive level it's terrifying to think these things can happen randomly, suddenly, to anyone—even to someone who is successful, relatively young, and "larger than life." In the face of this awful possibility we do what we have always done. We fight the darkness with stories. We smear magic paintings on cave walls.

If sick people need to find their voices, then so do those around them. My mother spent the last weeks on the phone, narrating his illness to friends and family, making a story out of something almost as soon as it happened. "The church was packed," she reported to a friend in Worcester after the funeral in North Carolina. "It was a glorious service and such a beautiful day." I wouldn't have been surprised to hear her brag that my father's death was a smashing success, and wouldn't have blamed her either. "She's being superficial," my younger sister accused. But what she was really doing was making sense of the senseless, fashioning a way to survive.

"What can I do to help?" everyone asks. Listen is the answer. Just listen and let people tell their stories.

I'd never realized that dying was such a social event, but it's obvious now why these rituals are in place: to give shape to things. I did my share of shaping, too, through everything I wrote. I felt guilty, but couldn't help myself. I needed it. I scribbled down notes while nursing him, or snuck away to write at the makeshift study I'd set up in my sister's old bedroom. Two hours before he died he looked over at me as I scribbled away in my journal. His lids were heavy and he hadn't said anything coherent in some time. "Make sure you get the facts down," he blurted.

The morning after he died, my mother admitted that she felt relieved—for him, of course, with all his pain—but for herself, also. I felt relieved, too. I dove back into my writing with full force. It felt wonderful. I wrote and wrote and wrote.

I don't feel guilty for that behavior, but I do for something else. The day before he died I did something inexcusable. I started writing about him in the past tense.

~

Two funerals in one week is a bit much, but here we are putting on suits and dresses, steeling ourselves. A few days back we filled a church in North Carolina, but today's service is for our New England friends. I'm all cried out, or so I think, but as soon as we arrive at the gravesite emotion overwhelms me. A bagpipe plays and people gather round near the oak tree. The fall weather has come in early. When the music stops the soughing of the oak leaves takes over. It sounds like a river, or creek, and silver trips off the sharp points of the leaves.

My brother didn't cry when my father died, and he has paid the price with temper tantrums and sullen silences. I try to imagine myself four years younger, with so much anger and so much un-resolved. Scott has been better since we got to the Cape. Now I feel proud of him as he reads his psalm in front of the crowd. He looks composed, dignified.

As for the preacher, he's young and earnest. He didn't know my father, and so can't capture his spirit. But one line from a psalm sticks with me. "We bustle about but all in vain," he reads. I scribble it down on the back of my hymn sheet.

We bustle about but all in vain.

Twenty minutes after my father died I went back into the den to say goodbye. If I thought about it at all, I suppose I imagined the moment would be a gentle one, but suddenly I found myself angry. You work to build things up, I said to him. You work and you work and then they kill you.

The next day I had to identify his body at the funeral home. His lips were bloated and his skin yellow. "Remember, it's not him," my mother said. But it is him, I thought. It is. This body is what he's become.

How do we live in the face of death? How can we put so much effort, so much energy into life when we each know our own ending?

I remember how hard my father worked on those jigsaw puz-zles right before we left the hospital at Duke. He loved to read but the morphine took that away, and so he turned to puzzles. With only an hour left before being discharged, we were a quarter of the way through a thousand-piece puzzle. There was no way he could finish, but he worked earnestly at his impossible task. "Just one more piece," he insisted.

Ultimately we will be interrupted, but we work and work. I think of the recent series of books about illness, writers who wrote in the face of death, working on novels and poems despite their sicknesses: Antole Broyard and Donald Hall in their books, Melvyn Bragg in interviews I've read. The natural thing would be to call these writers brave, but it's more than courage. It's necessity.

And that's what I take away from my father's death, that's the story I tell myself. There is no meaning, but we must live a necessary fiction. We must create our own meanings and live as if our lives depended on them.

I press flesh on the back of David Sears's deck. The funeral reception is in full swing and I feel as if I'm running for public office, shaking hands, telling one face my plans, moving on to the next face. They all want a piece of me—the men in particular—as if through me they can get a little of my father.

I drove here from the graveyard with my grandmother. She cried the whole way. She told me about the one time she saw him during his sickness. During his June stay on the Cape, she drove down from Worcester with my aunt to have lunch with him. But she couldn't make it through lunch. The sight of him overwhelmed her. She'd spoken to him almost every day on the phone, and she'd let the authority and command in his voice fool her. But then she saw him in the flesh. "There sat this thin, little old man," she cried.

At the reception I drink and consider the son my grandmother never knew. Around her he was always on his best behavior, eagle scout and Harvard boy. But here, on this deck, he was different.

Here, every July fourth, a crowd like this one would gather and watch him play the role of mad bomber. Fortified by a few drinks, he'd begin ripping into boxes of fireworks smuggled up from South Carolina. I remember him marching up the hill, carrying a paper tube about eighteen inches high, swinging it like a baton. He placed the tube on the ground and hunched down low over it, lighting a match that reflected red off his meaty face. When he knew the fuse had caught, he ran down the hill and dove for cover as if he'd unpinned a grenade. Then, as the rocket shot upward, he climbed to his feet and studied his creation. He beamed as the colored balls unfurled against the black sky.

There were cheers and whistles from the deck. They all knew the routine. His Fourth of July act was a tradition among our family and friends—ritualized, theatrical, Wagnerian. The crowd played their role well, cheering heartily or booing lustily at his pyrotechnic efforts, and my father fed off their reactions. If they cheered he'd throw his arms over his head and gloat in triumph; if they booed his shoulders would slump and he'd march back to his scoured launching pad, frowning with a little boy's glumness, vowing he'd show them this time. Over the years he did some strange things on July fourth, strange even by the bizarre standards of our peculiar family. Once he yelled "fuck" and slammed his forehead with his fist after one of his fountain rockets fizzled. Another time he responded to the boos by turning on the crowd and cursing them.

"You bastards!" he bellowed, shaking his fist with exaggerated fury. "*I'll show you bastards!*"

The audience responded appropriately with a round of savage catcalls, but when his next creation dutifully exploded and descended umbrella-like in streaming colors, the boos turned to loud cheers and he beamed.

One year I read the advertisement blurb on the side of one of his boxes of fireworks. "There's nothing like the light in a young boy's eyes when he watches Dad set off our rockets," it said.

"Which illusion do you choose?" asks Ernest Becker.

When I was young I learned my illusions from my father. I thought those illusions were straightforward: work and persistence; intensity to the point of madness; ambition. "The hunger of youth is for greatness," said Longinus. When I first got to college I vowed I would do something important. I decided I'd become a great political cartoonist.

I worked feverishly at my cartoons throughout college, swearing I would build the perfect Reagan. I got so absorbed that when

I took breaks I'd close my eyes and see Reagan's cocked head and jaunty smile on the screen of my inner eyelids. My various roommates stared as I hunched down over the drawings, decapitated presidential heads growing in a pile at my feet. After graduating I locked myself in the attic of the Cape house, working even harder at my cartoons.

What was I really doing up in that attic? I suppose creating my own swirling, romanticized world, using narcissism as a shield against death, trying to be like my father, or at least like my imagined picture of him. Later I turned the same energy toward writing. Samuel Johnson, despairing at the number of young writers chasing after fame, pointed to the thousands of unread books already crowding the libraries. He called this the "epidemic conspiracy for the destruction of paper." He was right, of course. If we stop and think, we are overwhelmed by the impossibility and absurdity of our tasks. But we can't stop to think. We put on blinders out of necessity.

I criticize the ambition and aggressiveness of the developers and builders on Cape Cod, but I'm the worse sort of hypocrite. Chris Cooney, a childhood friend, is one of those builders. He never went to college and moved naturally from mowing lawns as a teenager to a landscape business to a full-scale building operation. Who am I to blame him if he works hard at what he does? If I'd been pointed in that direction wouldn't I have worked just as hard at developing the Cape?

Finally, we leave the reception. Just the family—aunts, uncles, my young cousins—and two of my father's closest friends. The day's death rituals aren't quite over. We cremated my father at his request, and buried half his ashes at the graveyard back at Quivet neck. The other half come with us. We take the boat over to the Sears beach, where he spent a thousand summer afternoons. He was always the captain going outward, so today he once again takes the wheel. Bob Hunter rigs it with lines so that the silver urn, with a few adjustments, can handle the straight course to the beach. Someone cracks a Miller Lite and places it next to the urn. In the old days it would have been a Schlitz.

Despite its crassness, none of us think the gesture inappropriate. He would have liked it, we agree. We let the boat drift a hundred yards from shore and begin scattering the heavy gray ashes. The day is beautiful, the ocean still as a pond. As we take turns people start making impromptu speeches. More storytelling. My brother mentions *One Hundred Years of Solitude* and recalls asking my father whether he'd choose one intense year or one hundred mediocre ones. We all know the answer before Scott tells us.

Bob Hunter steers the boat back to the harbor. When we near the jetties, my cousins and I dive off and swim to the little beach. The sunset looks almost clichéd, a perfect orange ball dropping behind the water. My cousins run back to the house, happy. Uncle Dave will fade from their memories in no time.

Which illusion do we choose? We all create a fiction, of course, but our choice comes in which fiction we create. It doesn't take long to understand that work will not make us live forever, no matter how intense we are. Work will not beat death.

But that doesn't mean we shouldn't act like it does. Melville and Thoreau are long since mulch, but what a time they must have had writing their great books. A professor of mine complains that these days *everyone* is writing. Why not? It's a wonderful game to play while we're here—creating out of chaos—building jigsaw puzzles though we know we'll be leaving soon. To realize the absurdity of bustling and still to bustle. "To live is to play at the meaning of life," said Becker. If our meanings are make-believe, why not create the most exciting, compelling, and deep make-believe possible?

For a long while I misunderstood my father's make-believe. Work was only part of it. But our effort isn't very heroic if it's only turned inward.

Samuel Johnson spoke of "the hunger of imagination," of how our minds always gape and swallow, becoming colored by what we eat. We turn this constant energy toward envy, toward ambition, toward delusion, toward neurosis. But we can also turn it outward. Walter Jackson Bate, in his biography of Johnson, writes:

> the same outward leap of imagination that . . . leads us to look ahead to the next hour, the next month, to our future condition and interest (or that leads us back, with nostalgia, to the past) is also capable of

sympathetic identification with others, with moral values, or with anything else that can release man from the subjective prison cell of self.

Over the last few years I've finally begun to understand how much people meant to my father. I never saw this more clearly than at the end of his life. Two days after he died, his friends received their letters.

"What do you do with people who don't have anyone with them?" he asked a nurse in the hospital. "How awful that would be. I pass rooms with people alone in them and think how terrible this is."

That wasn't my father's fate. We all gathered around him at the end. Broyard writes about "beautiful deaths" and my father's was one. We chose the hospice route and so he died at home. During the last hour his liver failed and the pain finally ended. He began to breathe with a loud humming noise. All six family members and the cats sat on the rented hospital bed. He heard us tell him we loved him, heard us cry, felt us hold his hand and press up against him. We sat there as his breathing got slower, slower, and finally stopped.

My cousins return to the house and I stay on the beach alone. Walking out toward the bluff, the red of the sun runs in rivulets through the sand ripples. I listen to the quiet breathing of barnacles; they open like pores on the rocks. I follow a winding black trail of seaweed. Leading to the bluff.

Today the bluff shone half brown-purple, half spring green, the color in patches. Now it looms, hulking and dark. Freshets of water pour out of the grass behind Bagley's, off-flow from the cranberry bogs. It ripples down the dunes, heading back toward the ocean. When I turn home the windows of the houses behind me have become golden squares, abstract shapes floating in the air.

"I had several more lives to live," said Thoreau when he left Walden. My year is up. After a week with my mother, I head back to Colorado and unfinished business. But I'll be back, I'm sure of that. Like my father, I know where I'll finally settle. He has committed to Cape Cod. I will follow him.

UNIVERSITY PRESS OF NEW ENGLAND
publishes books under its own imprint and is the publisher for Brandeis
University Press, Dartmouth College, Middlebury College Press, University
of New Hampshire, Tufts University, and Wesleyan University Press.

ABOUT THE AUTHOR

David Gessner was born in 1961 in Cambridge, Massachusetts. He was raised
in Worcester and on Cape Cod. He received a B.A. in English and American
Literature from Harvard College, and completed an M.A. in creative writing
and English literature at the University of Colorado, Boulder. His writing and
caricatures have appeared in numerous newspapers and literary journals,
among them *Creative Nonfiction*, the Cape Cod *Times*, the Harvard *Crimson*,
Kinesis, and *Exquisite Corpse*, and his cartoons appear regularly in the Boulder *Weekly* and *High Country News*. Mr. Gessner lives and works in Boulder,
Colorado.

LIBRARY OF CONGRESS CATALOGING-IN-PUBLICATION DATA

Gessner, David, 1961–
    A wild, rank place: one year on Cape Cod / David Gessner.
        p.   cm.
    ISBN 0-87451-802-4 (cloth: alk. paper) ISBN 0-87451-803-2 (pbk.: alk.
paper)
    1. Gessner, David, 1961–   . 2. Cancer—Patients—Massachusetts—
Cape Cod—Biography.   3. Natural history—Massachusetts—Cape Cod.
I. Title.
RC265.6.G47   1997
362.1'96994—dc20
[B]   96-35908